Successful Teaching Placement
Primary and Early Years

Practical Handbooks

Achieving QTS

Successful Teaching Placement
Primary and Early Years

Jane Medwell
with Mary Briggs,
Julie Neale, Nigel Palmer
and George Raper

LearningMatters

First published in 2005 by Learning Matters Ltd.
Reprinted in 2006
Second edition published in 2007.

© 2007 Jane Medwell, Mary Briggs, Julie Neale, Nigel Palmer and George Raper

British Library Cataloguing in Publication Data
A CIP record for this book is available from the British Library.

ISBN 978 1 84445 091 6

The right of Jane Medwell, Mary Briggs, Julie Neale, Nigel Palmer and George Raper to be identified as the Authors of this Work has been asserted by them in accordance with the Copyright, Designs and Patents Act 1988.

Cover design by Code 5 Design Associates Ltd
Project management by Deer Park Productions, Tavistock, Devon
Typeset by PDQ Typesetting Ltd
Printed and bound in Great Britain by Cromwell Press Ltd, Trowbridge, Wiltshire
Learning Matters Ltd
33 Southernhay East
Exeter EX1 1NX
Tel: 01392 215560
info@learningmatters.co.uk
www.learningmatters.co.uk

Contents

Introduction

This book is intended for those who want to teach the Primary phase (5–11) including Key Stages 1 and 2, and those who aim to teach the Early Years (3–8) phase, including Foundation Key Stage and Key Stage 1.

To become a qualified teacher you need to obtain Qualified Teacher Status (QTS) and this is the goal of your Initial Teacher Training (ITT) and induction year. An important part of your training will be professional placements, which for Primary and Early Years take place mostly in nurseries, primary, junior, infant, first and some middle schools. In this book the term 'schools' covers all these settings and the term 'classroom' is used to encompass all the settings where teaching and learning take place.

Routes to QTS and professional placements in school

There are a number of routes you could take to obtain QTS and all are run by a training partnership, usually involving a group of schools and a university or Higher Education Institutes (HEI) but sometimes involving only schools. Throughout this book your training partnership will be referred to as the Initial Teacher Training Provider (ITTP). This book deals with the challenges you will face on all of the following routes to QTS.

The route undertaken by the largest number of trainees every year is the PGCE, which may be a Postgraduate Certificate in Education or a Professional Graduate Certificate in education. These are awards for those who have already completed a degree (or equivalent). If you do a Primary or Early Years PGCE course of any sort it is likely that at least half of it (minimum 18 weeks) will be spent in schools or nurseries. A large proportion of that time will be placements where you develop your teaching skills.

Not all postgraduate training is run by HEIs or universities. Some PGCE courses are delivered through School Centred Initial Teacher Training (SCITT). These courses, which may award a PGCE, are based in a school or group of schools and are accredited by a local University or HEI. If you do a course like this you may be spending most of your time in one base school and have teaching placements in that school and in others.

Some graduate training programmes do not carry the award of PGCE. Every year many mature trainees successfully complete the Graduate or Registered Teacher Training programme (G/RTP) and obtain QTS or the Overseas Trained Teacher Programme (OTTP). If you are following one of these routes you will spend most of your time in your base school and learn your subject knowledge and build up teaching skills gradually. You will also undertake teaching placements in your base school and in other schools.

If you have not already obtained your degree you may be undertaking an undergraduate degree course that includes QTS. This may be a two-, three- or four-year BA, BSc or BEd. The demands of an undergraduate degree are different from a PGCE because you also have study challenges to address – you are learning to be a successful learner as well as a teacher. However, you will undertake at least 24 weeks in school during a two- or three-year degree and 32 weeks for a four-year degree, most of the time on school placements.

These are the main routes into Primary (5–11) and Early Years (3–8) teaching but there are a number of other schemes to encourage people into ITT. This book will be useful to you, whatever your training route.

CASE STUDIES CASE STUDIES CASE STUDIES CASE STUDIES CASE STUDIES

Jane completed her first degree in French and German, travelled abroad for a year, worked for a charity running a play scheme and then began her Primary (5–11) PGCE. She did placements in Years 1 and 3 of a large city school and a longer placement in Year 5 of a suburban school. She has just completed her induction year and hopes to develop foreign language teaching in her junior school. Jane found her PGCE 'a really, really, tough year. But a fantastic experience with an incredible learning curve. I wouldn't have wanted any longer because after my long placement I was desperate to have a class of my own. To move the furniture and so on...'

Judy did a degree in biological science and was an environmental health officer for fifteen years. When her children went to secondary school she did a PGCE to re-train as a primary teacher. 'It was very demanding but I was ready for the challenge and the intensity (one year full-time) suited me. I have never regretted it. I found my first placement (in Year 2) awful but then went into Year 1 and Year 5 and loved both. I learnt that each class is very different...' Judy is an IT co-ordinator in a large city school.

Maureen had a career as a laboratory technician before her regular visits to her children's school attracted her to school-based work. She became a classroom assistant when her children started full-time school. After three years her head teacher persuaded her to do the GTP. 'I liked being part time and being in "my" school. At first it was hard to be taken seriously as a teacher when everyone was used to me as an assistant but my final placement in another school really helped me make the transition. I now work as an NQT [Newly Qualified Teacher] in the school where I trained and was once a classroom assistant. It's great – I feel real insight into what other staff do and I have learnt so much throughout my training.'

Andrew did a degree in Early Childhood and went straight on to an Early Years PGCE. He did placements in Year 2, Nursery and Reception – in three different schools. 'It was hard to learn the curriculum of both Key Stage 1 and Foundation Key Stage but it was really good to go into three Early Years settings. I feel I have an insight into the whole range and that helps not only the children but also my future promotion. My mentor on final placement gave me confidence and courage to go for a Reception job.' Andrew is an NQT in a Reception–Nursery unit, working with three teaching assistants.

Petra did a four-year BA with an English specialism. She did short placements in her first and second years in Year 3 and Year 1 in two different schools. In her third and fourth years, Petra had a Year 2 and a Year 6 placement in the same school. 'I started really slowly. I just had no idea what school was like from the teacher's side. But by my third year I was a totally different person. My knowledge of my subjects has changed out of all recognition and I've matured. I have learned so much and grown as a person on my placements and I feel I have grown into the role of the teacher. My mentors and class teachers were tireless in pushing me but also gave me the confidence I needed.' Petra is now an English co-ordinator in a suburban primary school.

The Professional Standards for Qualified Teacher Status (QTS) and professional placements

Whatever route you are taking through ITT you will be aiming to demonstrate that you have met the professional standards for recommendation for QTS, known as 'The Standards'. These are clearly set out in your course documentation and have three interrelated sections:

1. professional attributes;
2. professional knowledge and understanding;
3. professional skills.

You need to know these Standards really well as you will be using them to monitor your progress, set targets and shape your placements. You will have a chance to demonstrate most of the Standards during your professional placements.

Your course will be designed to enable you to demonstrate you have met these standards but the responsibility for collecting the evidence that you have met them is yours. You will be deeply involved in setting your targets, reviewing evidence and monitoring your progress. Your course handbook or guide will suggest formats and processes for doing this and each course is different. This book refers you to your course guidance whenever necessary.

The role of professional placements in ITT

The way each ITT provider plans courses is different but they involve many similar experiences. As part of your ITT you will probably experience some taught sessions in a university or training centre and may have school teachers from school coming to training centres to teach you. You will almost certainly be asked to audit and improve certain aspects of your subject knowledge through self-study. However, all routes to QTS have professional placements in schools (including Nurseries) as a central part of their training.

In schools you will be able to observe the way the subject knowledge you are acquiring is used and you will be able to see how teaching techniques are used. You will also learn about the culture and values of schools. These experiences are vital to all trainees. In school you will also be able to practise your planning, teaching and assessing, and the use of the subject knowledge you are developing. In school you will set targets for yourself and the children and assess and monitor your progress with feedback from at least one member of staff. Your mentor will be able to teach, direct and support you in improving your subject knowledge, planning, teaching and assessing – in short, to train you.

This raises a difficulty with terminology. Each training partnership uses its own terminology and your course may use terms such as 'supervised teaching practice', 'school experience', 'serial days', 'school visits', 'professional placement'. We use the term professional placement to identify a period when you are assigned chiefly to a particular class.

During a professional placement you will undertake a number of forms of training:

- **observation of particular children, class or group activities, aspects of management or teachers;**
- **planning;**

- **teaching and assessing pupils;**
- **reviewing your progress with feedback from staff;**
- **undertaking directed tasks;**
- **learning particular policies and curricula;**
- **taking part in meetings and in-service sessions.**

Many, but not all, of these experiences will be based in one class that you will get to know and teach for a substantial period of time. However, you will have some training needs that may require you to observe or teach in other classes or age phases and you will certainly want to develop your knowledge of progression and continuity through the age ranges. Professional placement is an important part of your training and offers training in all aspects of the Standards. It is important that you do not fall into the trap of thinking that professional placement is only a time to practise what you have learned elsewhere. There are key school staff who will participate in your training in school.

You will also have a *mentor*, a person assigned to oversee your training in school and participate in the assessment of your placement. The mentor will have been trained for his/her role. Your mentor may, or may not, be the same person as your *class teacher* who will work with you in your class and may participate in observing, advising and assessing you, as well as offering ongoing support. You may also have a *course tutor* (known as 'link tutor', 'adviser', or 'visiting tutor' in different courses) if you are involved in a course of teacher training. This is the person who may visit you in school.

Each person's ITT is unique and each trainee is different because you all have different experiences and different expertise. All training routes try to take this into account. You may have some experience of teaching in, perhaps, English as a Foreign Language (EFL) or a private school but find the demands of planning unfamiliar curricula challenging. Or you may be very familiar with the curriculum having been, say, a classroom assistant but find the management demands and performance aspect of teaching on placement a challenge. Each trainee will find some standards easier to address than others. This is why you will have some sort of *Individual Training Plan* to guide you through your course. This may be called a 'Professional Development Record', a 'training record' or something else. But it will be the document you use to set and monitor your targets. It will contain references to useful aspects of your prior experience as well as what you achieve during your training. Learning to use this sort of plan is important to succeeding in your ITT. It is also an important professional skill because you will have to do this sort of target setting and evidence collection throughout your NQT (Newly Qualified Teacher) year and the rest of your career.

Short placements

One special type of professional placement you may encounter will be the short visit to another educational setting. You may visit a secondary school to look at the secondary curriculum in action, or to focus on transition to secondary school. You might visit a Nursery to look at the transition issues involved. You might visit a school with a particularly good teacher of one subject, or good practice in teaching children with English as an Additional Language (EAL) or Special Educational Needs (SEN). If you visit these sessions for a very short period you will not be expected to teach in them but you will usually be given tasks to focus your attention on particular aspects of practice.

The responsibilities of professional placement

All those involved in professional placement (mentors, trainees, link tutors) take on responsibilities that are discussed in detail later in this book. One type of responsibility raises particular ethical issues – that is, your responsibility to the children in your class. When you are working in a class you are participating in the education of all the children in that class and they will not get that time, or even that lesson, again. You have a responsibility as a teacher from the moment you begin your ITT. This includes the responsibility to ensure the children are learning as they should. Your class have the right to expect that you know how to behave in school, are well prepared and are able to seek the help and support you need. This book will help you to be well prepared and knowledgeable.

QTS – your driving licence

The achievement of QTS may seem like a distant and demanding goal but remember it is also only a beginning. QTS is rather like a teacher's driving licence. When you achieve the standards for QTS you have achieved your driving licence and are safe to be let loose on a class relatively unsupervised. Like a novice driver, you are not an expert and will continue learning. Achieving QTS is a big step in your career but only the first step on a long road. It will be followed by a period of *induction*, further school-based training when you are an NQT, which you must complete within five years of your ITT.

In your ITT, try not to set yourself unreasonable demands. During professional placement you will find that you have to juggle demands, do extra research, fill gaps and generally cope with change. This is a normal part of school life and your training. Do not try to demand perfection of yourself and remember that you learn from the less successful experiences as well as the brilliant successes. Do not let off days (and you will have them) get you down.

PRACTICAL TASK PRACTICAL TASK **PRACTICAL TASK** PRACTICAL TASK **PRACTICAL TASK**

Before you go further in this book, you should review a number of important documents.

- **Your course handbook of guidance for your training. Check you know when the professional placements take place in your course and what is expected of you on each placement. Note anything that is unclear to discuss with your tutor or mentor at your next meeting.**

- **Look at your ITT plan. (This may be called a training record, record of professional development, monitoring file, etc.) As soon as you have started your ITT, this plan should contain background information about yourself, your targets and reports. Try to focus on what personal strengths you will be taking into your first placement.**

- **Look at the standards for the award of QTS (*www.tda.gov.uk*) and ensure you are familiar with them. Identify any that you are unclear about and look them up in the handbook of guidance (available from the same site) that gives further information about each standard.**

A SUMMARY OF **KEY POINTS**

> This book aims to help you to succeed at professional teaching placement in Foundation Key Stage, Key Stage 1 and Key Stage 2.

> If you are undertaking ITT, whatever your training provider, you will be doing professional placements.

> Your placement will involve an ITT provider, mentor, class teacher, and possibly a course tutor.

> Your placements will be guided by your own training plan (or record of development).

> As soon as you start your training you assume professional responsibilities and the first of these is to understand your training plan and the professional standards for the award of QTS.

Resources

Training and Development Agency for Schools. **www.tda.gov.uk/**. The TDA aims to develop a high quality, well trained workforce. Look at this site for information about training and induction requirements, financial support and all other aspects of training. You can find the Professional Standards for QTS here.

Teacher Training Recruitment Forum for Wales. **www.teachertrainingwales.org.** This site will give you information about teacher training in Wales, including the requirements which are slightly different from England. The site is in English as well as Welsh.

1
Preparing for professional placement

This chapter aims to make you aware of how your placements are organised, what is expected of you and what you can expect of those involved in your placement. The chapter is focused on helping you to prepare for a setting that is new to you.

By the end of this chapter you should:

- **know how and why teaching placements are selected;**
- **be able to research your placement school;**
- **be able to draft a letter to your school;**
- **know who will be closely involved in your training;**
- **be able to prepare a placement file;**
- **be able to join a teaching union.**

Selecting professional placements

All training partnerships running ITT will ensure you have placements in more than one school. This ensures you are prepared to teach in schools generally, rather than in just one particular school. It also offers you a much wider range of staff, children and resources to learn from. Here are some of the most frequently asked questions on this subject.

Frequently asked questions

1. 'How will my placements be selected?'

If you are pursuing a PGCE or BA/BEd/BSc programme, your ITT provider will assign places in the training partnership school on the basis of the information it has been given by you and by the school. So, if you are asked to fill in a form with personal details and questions about travel and domestic arrangements, make sure you are specific. ITT providers will accommodate you as conveniently as possible, taking into account the following factors:

- your training needs (the age phase or school type you need, any specific targets you have to address during this placement);
- the range of professional placement offers from schools in the partnership;
- the number of trainees who need placement;
- the geography and your travel arrangements;
- the training history of the school (you will not be placed in a school with a poor record of training or a school that has just gone into special measures);
- your commitments (if you are part-time, not all placements will be suitable).

Professional placement carries the same professional demands as other jobs. You may have to make domestic arrangements to ensure you can meet those commitments. It is not reasonable to expect placements to be arranged around pet care unless you are doing a part-time course.

If you are doing a GTP programme or SCITT based training, your base school will use similar considerations to place you appropriately for placements in other schools. Smaller partnerships may also want to take into account the need to swap trainees so that the arrangement is suitable for all schools.

2. 'Aren't all schools the same for placement purposes?'

Schools decide very carefully when they can best train trainees and the classes trainees can be placed in. Schools make offers based on that information and only offer to take a professional placement or GTP student when it will work for all those involved, including the children. These offers are always provisional, because schools are dynamic, changing places. A school may have a change of staff or particular year group that means they cannot take the trainees they had planned for.

3. 'There is a really convenient school at the end of my road. Why can't I just go there?'

All schools offering professional placement have to be part of the training partnership you are being trained in. If you are doing the GTP scheme, this may involve only two or three schools and if you are at university it may involve several hundred schools. However, each of these schools will share the same expectations of you, make similar demands and have staff trained to support you in particular ways. The convenient school you mention may not be in the training partnership.

Alternatively, the school you mention may be in the partnership but may want to work with trainees at a different time, not want a trainee at all this year or already have a trainee.

4. 'Why isn't the school at the end of my road in the training partnership?'

It is up to schools whether they join a training partnership. Most schools do, but this does not mean they can support placements every year. They may have a large number of NQTs or have school priorities that mean they cannot offer placements in one particular year. The school you mention may even belong to a different training partnership. Some schools are not in training partnerships. They may have school issues that mean they cannot participate, such as serious weaknesses they are addressing.

5. 'Can I choose my own school?'

Not usually. Your training school needs to be in the training partnership for the reasons discussed above. You are training to teach in all types of schools in your age phase, not just those you like. Your school must be chosen with a range of factors in mind and your training needs are the most important. This usually means you cannot choose. The only exception is where you do a GTP scheme in a particular school but even then you will be assigned to classes in your base school and to another school with your training needs and other factors or priorities. Do not approach schools yourself unless you are asked to do so – you may cause real professional offence.

6. 'I really liked Years 3 and 4 on my last placement. Why do I have to do Years 5 and 6 on this placement when I have already done juniors?'

One of your training needs may be to work right across the age phase for which you are training. In your case this is likely to be 5–11. You may need experience of Key Stage 1, lower Key Stage 2 and upper Key Stage 2. A whole placement in each is ideal but you may have to do some shorter periods in another year group during a placement if there is not time.

7. **'I am doing a PGCE and have been assigned a placement at some distance. My friend is doing a placement much nearer my home. Can we swap?'**

Check with the person who arranges placements. It may be possible to swap. But it may not, for good reasons. Either you or your friend may have training needs that dictate a need to place you in those schools. It may be that those schools can offer different age phases, or examples of particularly good practice. It may be that the travel arrangements of several trainees can be accommodated using this placement pattern. If the schools already know who to expect, changing places will cause inconvenience.

8. **'I will be doing a final placement in a school that has much more challenging behaviour than ours. Can I refuse this offer?'**

You are training to be a teacher who can teach in all Primary (or Early Years) schools. If this school is satisfactory in OFSTED terms and is part of the training partnership then it is probably a good training setting and you should take advantage of the training it offers. Remember, too, that a school in a challenging area may actually be very successful indeed and may offer you some excellent models of good practice. In this case you will have the chance to see successful behaviour policies in action and work with teachers who are used to this challenging setting – learn from the support they can give you.

PRACTICAL TASK PRACTICAL TASK **PRACTICAL TASK** PRACTICAL TASK **PRACTICAL TASK**

When you know which school you will be going to for your professional placement there are some things you should do before you visit the school.

Use the Internet to find out as much about the school as you can

- Search the OFSTED site for the school's most recent OFSTED report.
- How old is the OFSTED report? Does this mean some things will have changed, or that another OFSTED inspection is due?
- What weaknesses did OFSTED identify? These may well be areas the school will be working on and may particularly benefit you.
- Find out whether the school has a website and see what it tells you about the school. You might also check www.ukschoolguide.com – a website is a directory of all schools based in the UK.
- How large is the school? Does it have Key Stage 1 and Key Stage 2 and a Nursery? If you are aiming to look at transition between key stages this may offer you particular opportunities.
- What are the school's strengths? Some of these may be of particular interest to you.
- Does the school undertake particular events like residential trips that might affect you?

Check the location and travel arrangements for the school

If you are travelling to school by public transport, make the journey at the appropriate time of day before your placement. You can then make sure you allow enough time on the day itself. If you will be driving to school the same applies – check how long the journey actually takes; maps can be deceptive. When you know what your journey will be like you can make any domestic arrangements you need.

Explore the area around the school

When you get to the school take the time to explore the streets around it, ensuring that you choose a safe time to do so. Take a good look round so you can form some impressions about the lives of the children you will be teaching. You will also be able to identify what resources children will have experienced (such as shops, cafés, etc.) and what local features might be a part of your teaching (park, mosque, church, village hall, etc.).

Introduce yourself

When you know the name of your mentor (and head teacher) you may be advised to write to the school introducing yourself. Send your letter to the head teacher and the school mentor, to ensure it gets to the correct person. Schools increasingly communicate using email but it is always best to write a letter first, in case your school does not use email routinely. When you offer your contact details do provide as many as possible but be aware that if you offer an email address you must check it daily.

Your letter should not exceed two sides of A4 and we recommend less than one. Make sure you keep a copy to be included in your training plan or record of professional development.

Include:

- **your name, contact address, telephone number and email;**
- **degree subject and subject interests if you are a graduate or your A level subjects (or access) and subject focus if you are an undergraduate;**
- **your educational achievements;**
- **previous experience with children, including placements undertaken so far;**
- **work experience and particular skills gained from it;**
- **personal skills (like music, computing, sports);**
- **anything you think you could contribute to the school;**
- **what you would particularly like to achieve from this placement.**

Sample letter

Norma Smith
3, Chapel Hill, Coundon, Newcastle NE21 5BQ

Mrs Hughes
School Mentor
Manor Park School
Littleton Road
Newcastle

Dear Mrs Hughes,

I am writing to introduce myself before I meet you on 4 October on my first PGCE placement day.

I started the PGCE in Primary Education in September as a mature student and I have had a range of experience that I hope will be useful to me in becoming a teacher. After doing my degree in maths at Reading University, I worked for ten years as an accountant, mainly doing audits, before having my own children. My children's education introduced me to the world of children and I worked as a Play Assistant in a Nursery group and, for two years, as a classroom assistant in a Primary school. I found this role challenging and exciting and I think it has taught me a good deal about the importance of organisation as well as the need for flexibility in school. I was very pleased to be accepted on the PGCE and during the summer I worked hard to improve my subject knowledge, particularly in English.

On the PGCE course so far we have concentrated on the demands of teaching English, mathematics and science and I am keen to observe and teach these subjects. I am especially interested in making the most of the numeracy and literacy hours and I think my most immediate targets will relate to these. I am very interested in IT and I am looking forward to finding out about how your school uses the interactive whiteboards that I saw on the school website. I will bring my record of training with me on my serial visits and look forward to setting first placement targets during those days.

I will be coming to school on 4 October for the first of the three serial placement days. I will arrive at around 8.15 and I hope I will be able to meet you then. If this is not an appropriate time perhaps you could let me know.

Yours sincerely

Norma Smith

Join a union

Join at least one of the main teaching unions (we recommend joining all of them). All offer free membership to trainees and this includes valuable insurance and advice about all sorts of professional matters. Joining a union is discussed fully on page [20].

What to expect on your professional placement

When a school has accepted you for a professional placement, it has a commitment to ITT and is looking forward to training you during your placement. The training partnership will have a contract with the school that sets out what they can expect of you and what you can expect of the school. Look at your training programme or guidance and you will find this is set out for you. Each training partnership is different, so check your details carefully.

What to expect of your school

Some schools will have entered on a full partnership. This means that when you are in school you will be trained by and assessed by the school staff and school mentor. Other tutors from the university, HEI or Training and Development Agency (TDA) will occasionally come out to check arrangements and moderate assessments.

A partial partnership may be more complicated. The school staff and trained mentor will still take a good deal of responsibility for training and assessment in school but the assessment may be done wholly or partly with a tutor from a university, HEI or TDA. In this case you are likely to receive more visits from non-school staff as they will be taking part in your assessment and training in school.

MINI CASE MINI CASE MINI CASE **MINI CASE** MINI CASE MINI CASE **MINI CASE**

Maureen was a GTP trainee based in a training school in Coventry. Her school was in a full partnership.

During my GTP training I did placements in two classes in my base school and also a long placement in another school in a suburb of the city. During my training the school mentor met me fortnightly to discuss my progress, set and review targets and plan the training experiences I needed. I usually planned the agenda of those meetings and took the notes, but not always – we negotiated. These meetings were the backbone of my training and I continued them with the mentor in my final placement school, in a slightly different format.

I also had weekly observations on placement, with written feedback, mostly done by the school mentor and the class teachers of my placement classes. I also had observations and feedback from subject co-ordinators in the school, just as other teachers in the school did.

As a result of the observations and feedback I got I was able to take action to improve my subject knowledge and teaching. I used these observations and discussions to pinpoint what I needed to look up or what training course would benefit me. Sometimes very simple actions, such as reading school policies or discussions with other members of staff, brought significant training benefits for me – but some of these had to be identified in discussion. I'm not convinced I'd have thought of them on my own.

I was observed once by another mentor from the partnership in both my early placements and an external examiner came and observed me on my last placement. Although it was a bit stressful I found this reassuring and I was pleased that someone outside my immediate school was checking that my performance was comparable to others in my position.

My school mentor filled out my profiles (the assessment summaries of placements) and wrote the reports. I had to include these with my evidence file to get recommended for QTS.

MINI CASE MINI CASE MINI CASE **MINI CASE** MINI CASE MINI CASE **MINI CASE**

Ruth was a final year undergraduate trainee in a large primary school in Leamington Spa. Her school was in a full partnership.

I did my third year placement in two classes in the school (Years 1 and 2) and a fourth year placement in the Year 4 class. I had weekly meetings with my mentor at 2 p.m. every Friday. At these meetings we would look at three main things. Firstly, the observation and feedback from the observation that week, if there was one. Next we looked briefly at my targets for the placement and finally, we checked the standards to see which ones to prioritise for the next few weeks. In this way we always had a number of targets we could discuss. At our meetings I often came with questions I'd collected through the week because my mentor was not always accessible during the week and I didn't like to keep asking the other staff. I found I needed to write them down.

The mentor and class teacher did observations, mostly. The head teacher did observe me once and an OFSTED inspector too. It was nerve wracking but I felt I was more prepared than the other teachers because I was so used to having my teaching observed and commented upon. Sometimes we discussed the notes straight after the lesson but it wasn't always possible. Sometimes we had a quick talk after school.

My university link tutor came and observed once in each class on first placement and twice in the final placement. This was useful for me because I felt I got an objective view.

My mentor did my placement reports. These go into my record of professional development (training plan) as well as to the university and show that I passed the placement.

MINI CASE MINI CASE MINI CASE MINI CASE MINI CASE MINI CASE MINI CASE

Arshun was a PGCE (Primary) trainee who did his first placement in a very small chool near Plymouth. His school was in partial partnership and so he had more attention from his university tutor.

I basically saw my mentor all the time because I was in her class. She was a teaching head and I worked in her class with her and with the other teacher who shared the class. We planned meetings every week but, realistically, I think we met about once a fortnight (school activity permitting) which was plenty. She was very organised and had a focus for each meeting. Usually, this was an observation done of my teaching, or a particular aspect of teaching she wanted to draw to my attention, such as planning from the rolling programme or behaviour management. On a couple of occasions we scrapped the agenda just to talk about behaviour management because I was preoccupied by it then. I also had a specific meeting about a task the university had set me to complete on the placement.

I was observed by the other teacher in the class twice in the five weeks I was in the school. I also had two observations from the university link tutor who discussed them with me and helped me to identify points to improve and things I should do to help me keep developing. It was helpful to have their insights and my link tutor sometimes identified things I hadn't thought of.

When it came to assessment, the link tutor wrote a report and the mentor wrote a report. They talked to each other and to me in preparing these and there weren't any surprises.

What to expect of your school mentor

The standards emphasise that you should act upon advice and feedback and be open to coaching and mentoring for a good reason. This will be your chief vehicle of learning through professional placement. The school mentor will be a teacher who has undertaken training and takes a lead role in dealing with trainees in the school. Your mentor is crucial to your training on professional placement. In some schools your mentor may also be your class teacher, but often the mentor is a senior member of staff who can provide the sort of objective support that we all need from time to time. The role of the school mentor will vary depending on the level of partnership the school is engaged in, but in general you can expect the following.

Your mentor will:

- be your main point of contact with the school;
- know the school well, including the strengths of different members of staff, resources and opportunities;
- meet you on a regular basis to help you to set targets, evaluate progress, and identify experiences you want to have;
- know the professional standards for the QTS and how to help you demonstrate them;
- provide a link with the university or HEI, if you are engaged in a training course;
- be aware of your workload and help you to plan it effectively so that you can meet your training needs;
- observe some of your teaching and give feedback;
- assess and report on your progress; (In a full partnership school, the mentor is responsible for assessing you towards the end of the placement and filling out a full report or profile of your progress against the standards so far. In a partial partnership school the mentor may do this in conjunction with a tutor from a university or college.)
- be trained, know what to expect of trainees and pass information about trainees to other members of staff.

These roles are discussed more fully in Chapter 6.

Contacts

Your mentor will know the dates and expectations of the placement before you arrive. He or she may also have seen previous placement reports or subject knowledge reports from your course (if there is one) and will have limited knowledge about you. If you are on a GTP programme, your mentor will probably have spent time with you before you begin a long placement.

The mentor will also have a handbook of guidance for the placement as well as other training materials. However, it is a good idea to discuss the placement requirements clearly at the beginning. Mentors can help you to complete school-based tasks you may have been set as part of the placement or work you have to do for a project. Although they will know about these in advance you must discuss them with your mentor and plan when to complete them.

In school your mentor is the person who can provide details of the school policies, staff, etc. (see Chapter 6). Your mentor can also arrange training experiences you might need: perhaps observing a particular teacher who is good at something you are trying to get to grips with, or arranging a demonstration or discussion with an IT co-ordinator. If there is something you particularly need to be involved in, such as National Tests or report writing, you should always discuss it with the mentor, who will help you to make arrangements.

On your first day you should arrange to meet your mentor before school.

Planning, teaching assessment and recording

Your mentor will agree a timetable with you. This is not quite as specific as it sounds because of your developing needs and the pace of school life. At first your timetable will involve a great deal of observation. As you learn more about the class the amount of teaching will increase.

Your mentor will routinely plan for your involvement in the teaching of English, maths, science and ICT. Where you have targets that involve other subjects you will need to discuss these with your mentor and class teacher to ensure that, if they are not being taught in your class this term, you can go to another class.

Observation of your teaching

Mentors will manage and participate in observation of your teaching but they may not do it all themselves. Class teachers and subject co-ordinators may observe you teaching sessions and give you written and verbal feedback. Discuss who will observe you and when.

Regular review meetings

Your mentor will meet regularly with you to discuss:

- **observations and feedback;**
- **your performance against your targets;**
- **setting more specific targets;**

- your school-based tasks (if you have any);
- your performance against the standards for QTS.

Assessment

As your placement progresses your mentor will usually take the lead in writing a report about your progress. Different courses give these reports different names (profiles, reports, assessments, etc.). This report will be linked to the standards for QTS and will make judgements about the strengths and weaknesses of your teaching and subject knowledge based on the evidence provided by observation feedback sheets, mentor meetings, discussion, observations by other staff and the contents of your files. If you are engaged on a very long placement there will usually be an interim report about halfway through the placement. The report will be read by you, the mentor and any course staff involved in your training and will be the basis of target setting for subsequent placement, further course-based work or for your NQT year.

What to expect of the class teacher

Throughout your placement the class teacher will provide most of your day-to-day support. At the beginning of any placement, you will be observing your class teacher very closely to see how he or she works with the children, what the rules and expectations of classroom behaviour are and how your teacher rewards and enforces these expectations. Your first job is to be aware of these things and to get to know the names of the children in the class. You also need to know about your class teacher's routines and commitments in the school.

When you work with your class teacher he or she will be responsible for:

- showing you class rules and procedures (often by example);
- modelling good practice in teaching;
- helping you to analyse and reflect on your practice;
- focusing your attention on pupils' learning;
- discussing your planning so that it meets the school's needs as well as yours, and helping you to pitch it right.

Your class teacher may also:

- observe lessons on an agreed basis, possibly with your mentor or head teacher;
- give you written and oral feedback on your lessons;
- help you to develop self-evaluation strategies;
- monitor your files.

Your class teacher is your colleague, your model and your adviser. He or she will have a unique teaching style and by observing it you can learn valuable lessons. As you progress in your practice, the teacher will share lesson planning and share the teaching as well as supporting you in planning and teaching lessons.

What to expect of course tutors

The role of the course tutor in teacher training varies enormously from course to course and they have different titles – advisers, link tutors, visiting tutors, etc. You will need to be sure you know the structure of your course. Roles of the course tutors in placement may include:

- target-setting and approval;
- reviewing progress and targets;
- visiting the placement to observe your teaching and giving feedback;
- offering support for subject knowledge improvement;
- offering advice about teaching techniques;
- moderating mentor assessment and grading of your performance;
- offering support for the mentor in your training and assessment.

Target-setting or approval

In all courses you will be expected to set targets for your placement and agree these with either a course tutor or your school mentor. This is part of your personal professional development. These targets are discussed in more detail later, but you will be expected to link them to the standards for QTS. As you progress through your placement you will modify and add to your targets as you achieve some of them. See target-setting (Chapter 6).

Reviewing progress and targets

When you have completed a placement you need to review your progress against the targets you set and the standards for QTS. Use your placement report, any written feedback you have had, your file of plans and evaluations. Your course tutor may meet you to help you review the placement: if so, make sure you go to the meeting prepared. Make a frank assessment of whether or not you have met your targets and how well you have done. Identify the standards you still have to address. Consider your strengths and your weaknesses. As well as identifying targets, your tutors can help you identify what you should do to meet them. By engaging in this type of review you are addressing the standards for personal professional development (Q7a).

Visiting the placement, observing your teaching and giving feedback

Course tutors will usually arrange to visit you on placement at least once. There will probably be a number of reasons for the visit. They will want to monitor:

- that you are well placed and that the placement is meeting your needs;
- that you are making progress on your placement by building up your planning, teaching and assessment experience;
- that you are reviewing and achieving your targets;
- that you and your mentor are making the arrangements necessary to meet your targets;
- that you are doing any tasks you have been asked to do;
- that you are developing confidence;
- that your mentor is happy with your progress.

Support for subject knowledge improvement and teaching techniques

A visiting tutor may be able to suggest experiences you need to develop your teaching or subject knowledge. For instance, you might need to begin to teach the mental/oral section of a maths lesson, to observe National Tests in another year group or to discuss the Early Years Foundation Profile with the reception teacher. These arrangements can be made with your mentor.

Moderating mentor assessment and grading of your performance

On most courses, a tutor will visit to observe a lesson you are teaching. The tutor may do a joint observation with the mentor or teacher. This serves two purposes. First, the course tutor will offer you written feedback to assist your target-setting. Second, a joint observation will also have moderation value in the placement, ensuring that the tutor and mentor share opinions about your practice and expectations about what you should be achieving.

Support for the mentor

Course tutors will see many teachers and trainees teaching. They can help mentors to pinpoint the most effective experiences for you.

In some courses you may find these course roles split so that a personal tutor helps you set targets whilst an advisor visits you in school. Be sure you check the role of the course tutors in your placement for your particular course.

What the school is expecting of you

The school is committed to ITT so they are looking forward to your placement. The school mentor is expecting you to come to the placement with a professional attitude: most mentors would cite this as your most important quality. What is a professional attitude? It is the hallmark of a professional (of any type) that they aim to review and improve their work, develop their skills and abilities and take responsibility for their work and professional development.

- **You need to be enthusiastic and committed to your chosen training. Enthusiasm and commitment produce positive responses from staff and pupils alike.**
- **You need to show your enthusiasm and commitment by being well prepared and working hard. This will earn the respect and support of your colleagues and make your lessons go well. Nothing upsets colleagues more than a trainee who is constantly trying to avoid work or leave early.**
- **You need to be willing to ask for help and information in a polite and friendly manner, and to choose an appropriate person and moment to do so.**
- **You need to be sensitive to the stresses that all teachers occasionally feel – five minutes before a tricky lesson is not the time to ask the teacher of that lesson for help.**
- **You need to be reasonably self-critical and able to accept criticism and advice as a learning experience. No one learns without some less-than-perfect lessons. No one will expect you to have all the answers.**
- **You need to feel you are directing your training and balancing your needs with the needs of the teachers and children. No one will respect you if, at the end of a placement, you have not done specific tasks because you 'didn't get round to it'.**

Evidence of a professional attitude comes from a number of signs that you give in the early contacts with the school.

Appropriate dress is important. Different schools have different codes of dress for staff and these are usually unspoken rules. On your first visit it is worth being smart, but practical. Look at how the other teachers dress (perhaps on the school website). You will be setting an example to the children on behalf of the school and representing the school's values. Do not dress in a way that might upset children, parents or colleagues. Avoid immodest clothes and unusual hairstyles and remove obvious piercings. You will need to consider certain aspects of appearance for health and safety reasons. Long hair needs to be held back so that you have a clear all-round view, otherwise you cannot do the job. Your nails need to be short enough to help children in, say, gymnastics, without spiking them. Dress like a member of the profession you want to join but do not feel you have to be super smart or purchase a whole new wardrobe.

Punctuality is also extremely important. Although the children will probably arrive between 8.30 and 8.55 a.m., the staff will be arriving at school much earlier. If you arrange to arrive early at school in order to meet your mentor, he or she will have set aside some time for you. That time is precious so make sure you are there and ready to make the most of it.

Confidentiality is another important professional characteristic. As a trainee teacher you must show the same degree of confidentiality that is expected of other teachers. This means that what happens in school is confidential within the school. You can usually talk and write about school events within the training partnership. You would certainly want to do so in course essays, for example, but even then names of children, staff and schools should be disguised. You need to express yourself professionally and not make unsupported, sweeping or uninformed judgements.

In discussions within school you should avoid criticising your fellow teachers and gossiping about colleagues. This is just as important outside the staff group. Staff rooms contain a good many adults who are not members of school staff – visiting parents, advisers, inspectors, etc., and you need to remember this. You should not discuss school inappropriately with friends or relations

MINI CASE MINI CASE MINI CASE MINI CASE MINI CASE MINI CASE MINI CASE

The importance of confidentiality was brought home to Christine, a fourth-year BA student, in an uncomfortable way. Christine had undertaken a placement in the school the previous term and had discussed it with a friend whose child attended the placement school. At some point Christine unwittingly expressed a negative opinion of the teaching skills of Mr X. The following term Christine's friend approached the school and asked that her son should not be put into Mr X's class, because of what she had heard. Naturally, the head teacher of the school was very upset. She felt that Christine had acted unprofessionally and damaged the reputation of the school. Christine was aghast and realised that she had, unintentionally, acted extremely unprofessionally. This was certainly not the sort of evidence of team working and collaboration she wanted to accumulate towards meeting the standards. She could only write apologising to the school and learn a hard lesson.

All this seems a tall order at first, but as long as you go to school positive and well prepared, you will find your school welcoming. Your school has the right to expect you to come to a placement with:

- **a developing knowledge of the standards for QTS against which you will be assessed;**
- **an informed knowledge about your course of training – you should have read your course and placement handbooks;**
- **a clear idea of what your targets are for this placement; (On first placements this is much harder than in subsequent placements because everything is a target. Do not be afraid to discuss it with your mentor and set narrower targets such as specific observations or taking parts of lessons.)**

- a clear picture of what you want to get out if the placement, not just from the point of view of the course and the standards, but on a personal level;
- an expectation of participating in assessment and planning meetings;
- an expectation of participating in staff meetings and training days, although you may not have much to contribute at first;
- your training plan or record of professional development;
- a school placement file.

REFLECTIVE TASK

Prepare your documentation for school placement. You will usually have a school placement file and a file about your professional development such as a professional development plan or monitoring file. You might be asked to combine these.

Prepare your school placement file

This is a file that you will use day-to-day to hold notes on school policies, plans, evaluations, assessments, etc. At first your school placement file will not contain a great deal but it will indicate that you have given the placement some thought and begun your preparation. When setting up a placement file you need to read the course documentation very carefully and think about your targets. This will help you to decide the sections you will need in a file and how to arrange them. Before you get to school for a first placement a placement file may simply have the following:

- your details;
- details of the school (including OFSTED reports);
- file dividers for various sections (school policies, medium-term plans, weekly plans, daily plans, lesson evaluations, assessments, notes of mentor meetings, etc.);
- course details, including relevant sections of the course handbook;
- any forms needed for the placement, possibly as part of your record of professional development or training plan.

This is not in-depth material but it is a strong indicator of your attitude. A trainee who arranges this before the placement sends out strong messages of positive professional values like organisation. It shows you are committed and willing to work hard.

Prepare your training plan file (or professional development profile)

This document will have your background details in it, the standards for QTS and will develop to form a full record of your training. This file will probably be where you record the targets you set for the placement with the mentor or link tutor. At the start of a placement you should expect to spend some time reviewing this record. Use the format you are given as part of your training to:

- identify what you have already achieved in relation to the standards;
- identify key standards which you aim to meet (Q7a).

You will discuss your record with your mentor at the school of the placement.

You will do a good deal more with this file after the placement, when you may want to put lesson plans, lesson observations, assessments and photographs into it.

Union membership

Most teachers belong to one of the main teaching unions (contact details on page 139). These are trade unions that negotiate on behalf of their members on issues such as pay and conditions. However the unions also offer a wider range of additional services. Most of the unions produce materials especially for trainee teachers and NQTs. These range from advice about classroom management to tips for getting a job. The publications are often free to trainees and many trainees have found them invaluable. The unions also offer services such as insurance cover as part of membership. Each package is different but may provide insurance cover for:

- **personal accidents;**
- **hospitalisation;**
- **personal property (including spectacles);**
- **malicious damage to motor vehicles in school or college premises.**

The membership may also include the union's legal services in the case of any dispute and the services of the union in agreeing your pay package when you take up a job.
There are also additional benefits such as:

- **discount shopping;**
- **life assurance and investments;**
- **mortgage facilities;**
- **legal services;**
- **credit card facilities;**
- **personal loans;**
- **motor insurance;**
- **motor breakdown and recovery services;**
- **travel facilities;**
- **tax recovery services;**
- **magazines;**
- **pocket diaries, calendars and pens, etc.**

We strongly recommend you join at least one union before going into school for the insurance benefits as well as the excellent advice. Membership is usually free for trainees and some NQTs. Each union has slightly different policies and, eventually, you will want to be a member of a union that represents your view but, as a trainee, you do not have to make a final decision about which union because you can join them all. If you are doing a PGCE or degree course, the training HEI or university may well have arranged contact with the unions. If not, they can be contacted at the URLs listed below.

The unions will have local branches and you may find that in many schools all the staff belong to one union but you can decide about this when you are an NQT.

MINI CASE MINI CASE **MINI CASE** **MINI CASE** MINI CASE **MINI CASE** **MINI CASE**

I only joined the unions because they were all there in the university one day and they were giving out good leaflets and pens and I really didn't expect to need them. On my very first placement my car was badly scratched in the school car park. On placement you are quite tense anyway and I found it really upsetting. I had already had a recent insurance claim and risked losing my no claims bonus if I claimed on the car policy. I also didn't want to make a fuss in school or draw attention to myself. The union said I was covered through them and they paid out for the repairs with very little effort on my part. Since then I have had the magazines and booklets they send, which have been good, especially in helping me to prepare interviews. I also consulted them about my starting salary. I will retain membership of all three unions this (my NQT) year then decide which to go for when I have to pay.

Nahid, NQT

A SUMMARY OF **KEY POINTS**

> **Your placements are chosen with your training needs and circumstances in mind and should include a range of experiences for you.**
> **You should do a little research about your school before you start.**
> **You should write to your placement school and introduce yourself as a professional, enthusiastic trainee.**
> **Your mentor is a member of the school staff who will know about your training and will work to support you through your placement.**
> **Your class teacher will be your principle model of good practice and will teach with you.**
> **Course tutors (if you have them) will participate in your training, moderating, offering advice and training.**
> **From the very beginning of your placement you must act professionally. This means having a professional attitude, being punctual, maintaining confidentiality and dressing appropriately.**
> **We strongly suggest you join at least one teaching union before beginning placement.**

Resources

Association of Teachers and Lecturers **www.atl.org.uk**. ATL, formerly the Assistant Masters and Mistresses Association (AMMA), is a fully democratic, TUC-affiliated trade union and professional association.

Educational Institute of Scotland **www.eis.org.uk/**. The EIS is the largest organisation of teachers and lecturers in Scotland representing around 80 per cent of the profession in nursery, primary, special, secondary and further and higher education.

National Association of School Masters/Union of Women Teachers **www.teachersunion.org.uk**. NASUWT is one of the largest teaching unions and the only one to organise in England, Wales, Scotland and Northern Ireland. NASUWT has members in all sectors of education and represents teachers in all roles including heads and deputies.

National Union of Teachers **www.teachers.org.uk/index.php**. The NUT is the largest of all the teaching unions. It is a professional association and a trade union that also provides access to a variety of conferences and reference materials for teachers and staff within the education sector. Membership for students is free.

Professional Association of Teachers **www.pat.org.uk**/. This independent trade union caters for all workers in education. Founded in 1970 it has approximately 35,000 members.

Teachernet www.teachernet.gov.uk/professionaldevelopment/professionalassociations/unions. Teachernet is the DfES site for teachers. it contains information for teachers about all aspects of professional life. You can link to all the unions from this site.

2
Starting in school

In this chapter we aim to help you gather information in a setting that is new to you. Even if you have considerable experience in schools you may benefit from taking a close look at the culture and organisation.

By the end of this chapter you should:

- **know the purpose of preparation days;**
- **know what to find out about your school;**
- **know what information to collect about your class;**
- **be able to observe in the first days in your class.**

Placement preparation days in school

Before you start the main body of a professional placement, or at the start of that placement, you will spend a few days in the school to get used to the setting. This may be one day a week for several weeks or it may be a few days in a single week. On a school-based programme you may have been in school for some time and will really be focusing on the new class or age phase. However your preparation time is organised, this time is crucial in enabling you to be ready to make the most of a professional placement.

In those first few days it is important to get to know the school and you should expect members of staff to help you to do that. The school mentor will arrange the first few days in a new situation so that you can:

- **tour the school, perhaps with children;**
- **have a copy of the school prospectus;**
- **learn tips about the school routines (such as timetables, playground duty, etc.);**
- **learn the rules for photocopying and use of resources;**
- **see and note the school behaviour and Health and Safety policies;**
- **learn the first aid procedures;**
- **learn the fire drill procedures (for your class);**
- **set up regular mentor meeting times;**
- **learn about your class.**

Many schools will have a trainee teacher induction pack ready for you. This usually includes:

- **the school prospectus;**
- **guidance given to supply teachers about routines, break times, etc., school behaviour and health and safety policies;**
- **a staff list;**
- **a school map.**

If your school does not have such a pack you should ask your mentor for access to these documents.

School layout and emergency exits

It is usual practice for the school mentor to show students around a school on an initial visit but in a large school this can leave you feeling overwhelmed by the sheer amount of information given. It is a good idea to obtain a copy of the school map and ask a small group of older children to take you on an additional tour during a lunch break. In this way you can proceed at your own pace and annotate the map with any notes that will be personally useful. It is also crucial that you know the location of fire exits of the area you will be working in and your assembly point outside the building. Identify these on the map and clarify the procedure for using them with your class teacher. You can build on this information by looking at the school health and safety policy.

Who's who?

When you join a school for a teaching placement you become a member of the school team, even if you are a temporary, junior member. Make a conscious effort to become acquainted with not only your class teacher but with other staff too. The school staffing list may be extensive, so make short notes next to names to help you remember who's who. Try to learn names, starting with those of your mentor, teacher, teaching assistant(s) and head teacher and notice how staff members address each other – it would be unfortunate to call your head teacher by his first name if the class teacher always calls him Mr – . A little polite conversation will usually allow you to find out what your mentor's and class teacher's areas of responsibility are within the school, what age group or sets they teach and which parts of their work they enjoy most.

It is essential to know the names and roles of any parallel class teachers and support staff. You will be working closely with them – observing their practice, planning, sharing resources – and may teach lessons with them. You will also want to learn the names of a wider circle of teachers over the first week or so of the placement. The SENCO (Special Educational Needs Co-ordinator) will be an important member of staff who can tell you about processes for children with SEN, show you some Individual Education Plans (IEPs) and discuss arrangements made to meet the needs of a range of children. There will also be subject co-ordinators for each subject in the Primary curriculum and for the areas of learning at Foundation Key Stage. Knowing and understanding the roles of colleagues with specific responsibilities is part of the standards (Q20). You may want to learn from these members of staff later in the placement by, for instance, observing particularly good guided reading by the literacy co-ordinator or a dance lesson led by the PE co-ordinator. Arrangements of this type are usually made through your mentor and you should discuss them with the mentor in the first instance.

Look beyond the classroom and introduce yourself to staff in the office and the lunchtime supervisors who work directly with the children. This will allow you to appreciate the school community properly and established, knowledgeable staff are more likely to support and advise a student who makes an effort to be friendly than one who shuts themselves away in their classroom.

Important routines – assemblies, playground duties and lunchtime

One of the most important, and obvious, pieces of information you need is the timing of the school day. This information may well be in your welcome pack but if it is not, make sure you note on your first day:

- **school starting and finishing times;**
- **when staff arrive and leave the school;**
- **the times of break times and lunchtime;**
- **assembly times;**
- **the weekly staff meeting time;**
- **any regular phase or planning meetings.**

These form the basic structure of the day but you will also want to observe the teachers' routines over your first week. Most teachers arrive some time before the children start and leave some time after school finishes. They will all stay on to attend the weekly staff meeting. You should expect to do the same and you may well find that, early in your career, you need extra time to accomplish your preparation. If your school has staff training days for the whole school staff it is important that you take part in these, although as a trainee you should expect to keep a low profile. Participating in these aspects of school life shows your professional commitment.

Try to observe and learn the school's social rituals. On your first day ask what the arrangements are for paying for coffee and tea and offer to contribute. Notice when the teachers congregate in the staff room and when they stay in their rooms to prepare. There will not be time for you to leave school premises during the day. Do not expect to be able to pop out to the shops at lunchtime or make personal arrangements during school time. If school staff bring a packed lunch or have school dinners, do the same. Most teachers spend a very short time in the staff room at lunchtime but they will usually choose the same times to do their preparation and all use the beginning, middle or end part of lunchtime to congregate in the staff room. It is important to participate gradually in these routines. In a Nursery there may be very little time at break time or lunchtime and staff may have a rota for these occasions. It is important to notice when the staff do meet to chat and mentors will see your willingness to participate as part of Standard Q32 – working as a team member.

There will be wider opportunities for child-orientated activities. Breakfast and after-school clubs are common and you should find out about them. You will also, gradually, want to find out about and after school or lunchtime activities. Your knowledge of French, chess, rugby or line dancing might be useful and allow you to contribute later in the placement.

MINI **CASE** MINI CASE MINI CASE **MINI CASE** MINI CASE MINI CASE **MINI CASE**

We'd all made the usual jokes about not sitting in the deputy head's chair before the placement but, really, going into the staff room for the first couple of times on all my placements was a bit nerve-wracking. My first school was huge and the staff room seemed vast. I felt very conspicuous. Everyone pretty much ignored me and just made their own tea and put the cups in the dishwasher. My mentor sort of waved me on and said 'help yourself'. I didn't say a word for the first few times in there but gradually I found I could join in the general chit chat. The staff sort of included me and I can see, looking back, that their lack of fuss was actually reassuring. I didn't spend much time in the staff room – about 15-20 minutes at lunchtime, maximum – but after five weeks I was really at home. I see now how important it was to be part of the staff in that way.

Jennie, PGCE.

MINI CASE MINI CASE MINI CASE **MINI CASE** MINI CASE MINI CASE **MINI CASE**

I had been a TA, so I was used to schools but I did find I talked about different things in the staff room during my placements. In a few minutes at lunchtime I could ask all sorts of things and sort out resources. I enjoyed the familiarity but it felt different.

John, GTP.

MINI CASE MINI CASE MINI CASE **MINI CASE** MINI CASE MINI CASE **MINI CASE**

My placement was in a nursery school so even with the nursery nurses and teachers on a rota there were only really three of us in the staff room at lunchtime or on breaks. I was surprised that this worked so well, but it did mean that planning meetings were even more important. I think that it is really vital to remember to take your breaks for tea and keep your energy levels up.

Pat, BA.

All teachers are involved in some routine duties such as playground or corridor supervision or bus loading duties. These are important times for supervision of the children but most of all a very important time for you to see the children outside the very formal setting of the class. You should go with your class teacher when they do these duties. If they do not do playground duty, arrange through your mentor to go out with another teacher.

PRACTICAL TASK PRACTICAL TASK PRACTICAL TASK PRACTICAL TASK PRACTICAL TASK

Do a playground duty with another teacher (Key Stage 1 or 2). Choose a day when you have already met your class and know them a little.

As you go out ask:

- **How often does the teacher do playground duty?**
- **What is his/her main purpose in doing duty?**
- **What are the behaviour rules for children in the playground?**
- **What, if any, equipment is provided?**
- **Who is the first-aider and what is the procedure for cuts and grazes?**

Notice how the teacher circulates round the area and talks to groups of children.

- **How does the teacher appear friendly with them?**
- **How does the teacher, at the same time, maintain a professional relationship?**

You need actively to imitate these strategies so that the children will chat with you but not be too familiar. You should discourage gratuitous cuddling, children's hands in your pockets and over-personal questions. Children will try these as ways to test your role as a teacher.

Observe the children at play. For many of them, playtime is the most important part of the day and it is certainly the time when most social learning is going on – how to make and keep friends, turn taking, joining and leaving groups, negotiation and compromise. Playtime may also involve a little mild violence or psychological torture (mostly about friendship) and you have a role here in preventing bullying and helping children to sort things out.

Observe what the children do at playtime.

- **Do different groups do different things?**
- **Does there seem to be a difference in activity related to age or gender?**
- **Look at children you know and see who plays together.**
- **Are there any children on their own? Do they seem happy?**
- **Who complains of being left out? How can you help them to take part?**
- **Are the children using the equipment – climbing toys, sand pits, markings, skipping ropes, etc?**
- **Which children use them?**
- **What games are being played (ball rhymes, skipping rhymes, variations on tag, etc.)?**

Observing your class in the playground can give you a much greater understanding of some children.

Moving around the school and class

Notice how the children move around the school. This is a very rule-governed business and recognising the rules (and when someone is breaking them) is one of the things that identifies you as a teacher to the children. On your first day notice how the children use the corridors (no running, letting others pass nicely) and be prepared to ask children to do this.

There are also basic rules for moving around in your class.

- In an Early Childhood setting, what are the processes for settling children on the mat?
- In a nursery setting, what are the rules for behaviour on the mat?
- During seatwork, when are the children allowed to leave their seats?
- When they are sent to get an item in class, how are they supposed to move, and what are the sanctions for running, etc?
- When you want to accomplish a transition such as moving from the mat to groups, what is the procedure and best way to give instructions?
- What key words should you include in instructions to move around?
- When the teacher sends children to get something, note how he or she avoids all the children rushing to the same place.
- What procedure is used when moving into another class or area? Do the children line up?
- When moving into the hall for PE, do the children do something specific, like finding a space?
- When the teacher sends a child to another place with a message, register or other task, what is the routine? Is it a privileged job? Does more than one child always go?

These are small but important details and observing them will establish your role as a teacher.

MINI CASE MINI CASE MINI CASE MINI CASE MINI CASE MINI CASE MINI CASE

In my first placement I didn't really establish myself with the class and I felt they saw me as a helper – not a teacher at all. It shrivelled my confidence. On my next placement I asked my next mentor for advice before I even went into class. She told me to start by moving groups around as part of the lessons my teacher was teaching that day. I worked with my teacher to do this on my second day. It set me up. I began by showing a bit of authority, with my teacher there to support me, and I built on it. On my third day I lined the class up and took them into the hall for assembly. It took a bit of time to get silence and some naming of individuals to keep it but I felt it was the one act that established my role and set me up for really teaching that class.

Abby, Second Year BA.

Taking photographs in school

A small but important aspect of your ICT work will be taking photographs in school. As part of your assessment evidence, especially at the Foundation Key Stage you (and the children) may well take photographs of children and you will certainly take photographs of assemblies and school visits. These photographs can be shared with the children for discussion, discussed with parents and may go into displays, children's work and school newsletters and websites. The use of photographs is governed by the school policy and professional responsibility. The school will have a policy about the use of photographs that aims to protect the identity of children and of the school. You must read it and adhere to it.

You should also ask your teacher to take photographs of you teaching in a way that adheres to the school photography policy. Photographs of you teaching a class masterfully, using the interactive whiteboard, working sensitively in the dramatic play area, reading with a group, accompanying a school visit or assisting at cookery are not only excellent in supporting your evidence towards the standards for QTS, but also go down very well at interviews for teaching posts.

When you use photographs of yourself teaching for displays, ensure that all children are not identifiable and that the school name cannot be identified from the photographs. If it is on the school sweatshirt you may have an interesting ICT challenge smudging this part of the image.

Your class group(s)

On your placement you will have a key teacher and class but this might mean different things in different placements.

Early Years settings have a number of different ways of organising their work. All of them will involve teachers and nursery practitioners planning together and teaching together.

- **Nursery classes can be an ordinary class in the school with a nursery teacher and nursery nurse.**
- **Nursery classes may be part-time or have two shifts of children, those who come in the morning and those who come in the afternoon, with a few who stay all day.**
- **Early childhood settings may be organised as Foundation Key Stage units. This might mean a combined Nursery and Reception unit in which all the children from both years work together. These units may have two teachers and a number of nursery practitioners or one teacher and more nursery practitioners.**

Whatever the organisation, you will be assigned to one teacher and will be gradually taking over his or her role in the planning, teaching, management and assessment of this class. For Early Years this means working very closely with the team of nursery practitioners or teaching assistants and you will have to be very careful to identify the teacher's special role in the team. This is not as easy as it sounds.

In Key Stage 1 placements you may find a number of ways of organising classes. Classes will not exceed 30 children, and most of them will have a single teacher and a part-time or full-time teaching assistant.

- **A simple Year 1 or Year 2 class with one teacher is probably the most common organisation.**
- **Many classes will be mixed years, with Reception children (who are doing the Early Years Foundation Stage curriculum) and Year 1, or Year 1 and Year 2 together. Mixed year groups make planning a little more challenging.**
- **Some schools choose vertical or family grouping as a matter of principle. In these schools there may be a number of Key Stage 1 classes all organised to include Year 1, Year 2 and sometimes Year 3 children.**
- **In a very few Key Stage 1 settings, usually in larger schools with multiple form entry, there will be sets where children are re-grouped across the classes for a particular subject (often mathematics or English). You will usually work with the sets your teacher takes and have the extra challenge of getting to know a larger number of children.**
- **Some larger Key Stage 1 settings may organise the children into home groups with a teacher responsible for up to 30 children but the curriculum will be organised over a number of rooms or areas such as the literacy area, maths area, creative area, etc. Each teacher may plan for and teach one area. In this case you will stick with your teacher for home group time and work in different areas at different times to get experience across the curriculum.**

In Key Stage 2 you may have classes of over 30 pupils. Each class has a teacher and some time from a classroom assistant. You may have:

- **a single year class that does all subjects with the teacher;**
- **a single year class that does most subjects with the teacher but has some specialist teaching in music, PE or some other subject;**
- **a mixed year class that may do all subjects, or some with the same teacher;**
- **mixed year or single year classes that set for English, mathematics and sometimes science. This is very common in Key Stage 2, especially in schools with more than one form entry. In practice it means that the children all go to pre-arranged classes for mathematics and English at an agreed time. The sets may be organised by ability and children may be in different sets for English and mathematics. You will usually work with the set for which your class teacher has responsibility but your training needs might require that you work with a different set. For example, if you wanted to develop your differentiation for able pupils, you might work with a top set.**

Meeting the class

Whatever class you are placed in, your first step will be meeting the class teacher and simply watching the class for a day, perhaps helping children to complete tasks. Your introduction to the class is very important. The children will use your title and surname (unless first names are used for all teachers in the school) and the teacher will tell the children you will be teaching them for some of this term. You must look confident and relaxed, however terrified you feel, and fill the role of teacher as you are introduced. Stand up straight and keep your arms relaxed (it may help to hold a file or something to stop you nervously clasping your hands). Smile – a relaxed, authoritative smile is appropriate, not a nervous whimper or a rictus grin. Any time you say something it must be confident and authoritative: 'I am looking forward to teaching you' rather than a weak 'Hello'. First impressions count and you need to signal to the class that you know what you are doing – even if you are not really that sure of yourself.

During your initial visits, obtain class lists for all the groups of children you will be working with. Then take time to annotate these lists from your observations and in discussion with the class teacher. His or her observations will be very useful and enable you to begin to formulate a class picture before actually working with the children. The checklist below suggests possible queries for you to observe or discuss with your class teacher.

- **How many children are there in the class?**
- **Who is full-time/part-time/morning or afternoon (for nursery)?**
- **What sets are there and who is in which?**
- **How are the class seated? Do they choose a spot or are they assigned chairs? If they generally stay in the same places, making a seating map will help you learn names.**
- **Which children are on the school's SEN register? How does their special need manifest itself? How does the class teacher plan for inclusion?**
- **Which children in the class have been identified as gifted and talented on the school's register? In which subject(s) is the child gifted or talented? What strategies does the class teacher utilise to ensure they are reaching their full potential?**
- **Which children have EAL? What other language do they speak? What arrangements are made to support them?**
- **Which children find difficulty in controlling their behaviour? Is this related to an identified SEN? What steps does the class teacher take to manage the child's behaviour? Is there a reward system? What will happen if the child needs to be removed from the classroom as a result of its behaviour?**
- **Are there any sensitive issues about any child's family circumstances you need to be aware of (e.g. recent bereavement, divorce, parental custody or child protection concerns)? Remember you are expected to treat this information with the highest degree of confidentiality.**
- **Are there any children with medical problems that you should be aware of? For example are there any children with asthma, epilepsy or allergies? Where are the inhalers kept? Who is qualified to administer a child's epi-pen? Who are the school's first-aiders? What procedure should you follow if a medical incident occurs during your lesson?**
- **Which friendship groupings are conducive to learning and which are not?**
- **What teaching assistance does the teacher have? When do teaching assistants work with the class? When do teaching assistants work with particular children? What are the roles of teaching assistants in this class? Are there any other adults working in the class?**

As you spend your first day in the class you will begin to learn children's names and to see how they work.

PRACTICAL TASK PRACTICAL TASK **PRACTICAL TASK** PRACTICAL TASK **PRACTICAL TASK**

Observe a daily routine. On the first day in school you need to note as many class routines as you can. Use one of these question lists to guide your first observations, then supplement these in discussion with your teacher. Make a note of times at each transition point.

Early Years setting

- How (and when) do the children come into the building?
- How do staff greet parents and how long do parents stay?
- Is the first activity of the day set up? When? By whom?
- How do children know where to go?
- Which adults manage which tasks? Who is outside?
- Are outdoor clothes such as wellington boots and coats used? What is the routine?
- How do adults participate in play tasks?
- How is a change of task signalled? (Music, clapping, hands in air, etc.)
- How many children are allowed to do each activity at a time? How do they know?
- What is the routine for fruit time? Who prepares it? What do the children do? What language is used?
- What are the routines for using the lavatory and hand washing? (If any children in the setting wear nappies, ask your teacher for advice.)
- When do the children gather for group (or class) time on the mat?
- What do children do for packing up time? How is this signalled?
- When are stories and rhyme routines done?
- What arrangements are there for children taking books home (or story sacks) and changing them?

Key Stage 1 or 2

- How (and when) do children come in from the playground and what are they expected to do as they come in?
- How does the teacher settle the class to attention?
- Who takes the register? How do children respond? What do the children do as it is taken? What happens to the register?
- Is there an assembly? Does the teacher attend?
- What are the lesson times?
- How does each lesson start and finish?
- Which other adults work in the class during teaching times and what do they do?
- How are resources (pencils, books, etc.) arranged? Who collects them?
- How does the teacher get the children's attention?
- How does the teacher move children from the mat to tables?

Timetable, curriculum, resources and behaviour

In your first few days you will have the chance to talk to your mentor and your teacher.

Your mentor will play a lead role in the school's involvement in the partnership for training. This means the mentor will be familiar with the standards for QTS, even if the rest of the staff are not. Your mentor will also have contact with the HEI involved in your training (if there is one) or the TDA if you are on a GTP programme. So your mentor will know the arrangements for your placement and the requirements (generally) of this placement – which key stage you need to be in, when you will be arriving and something of your previous experience. The mentor will also know their role in helping you to become established, observing, arranging meetings with you and reviewing progress. Usually, the mentor will have the report forms that may be required about your progress, but in some courses you will take these into school yourself.

The mentor may have some reports on your previous placements and you may have sent a letter about yourself. Your mentor will be keen to know a little more about you and will certainly want to set, or see, specific targets for this placement. On some courses, you may decide on these with a course tutor before the placement. In others you will set these with the mentor early in the placement. Either way, meeting these targets, showing your mentor evidence that you have met the targets, and setting new targets are important elements of your relationship. So your first mentor meeting will focus on:

- **discussing the requirements for the placement and personal targets for your placement;**
- **helping you to get information about the school;**
- **answering your questions so far.**

You will also meet your teacher. Key topics for discussion with him/her will be the timetable of the class, planning for class teaching and managing behaviour.

Having observed a day in Key Stage 1 or 2, you will have ideas about the rough timings of the day. To draw up a timetable you need to check these and add hall and PE times, times when any sets meet, times when the class is booked into an ICT suite and times when other teachers take the class. You can then put in the teacher's intended teaching times. These may be simply English, mathematics and cross-curricular themes, or each subject may have an identified time. Many schools block some subjects into different terms, so your class may do art one term and design and technology (D&T) the next. You will also need to know what teaching assistance you have in and out of the classroom and who will work with children during your lessons.

In Early Years Foundation Stage you will have a broad idea of the pattern of activity from observation and you need to discuss with the teacher how the six areas of learning are addressed. Do different staff manage different areas? Does each member of staff plan activities for each area? You need to know which activities the children are encouraged to do and which are a matter of choice. How is this monitored?

The planning of the teaching is your next area of interest. Establish what topics are to be taught and what associated learning objectives need to be achieved in each curriculum subject during your placement. Obtain copies of any relevant medium- and short-term plans and look at these with your class teacher. He or she will identify lessons for you to observe and be sure you know whether you are expected to take part in them. Planning is discussed in more detail in Chapter 3.

When you have identified the lessons, or parts of lessons, you will teach on the timetable, it is essential to be prepared. The following checklist will help.

- **Find out where the school stores the curriculum resources (this will take a little time). Which resources are classroom based and which are kept centrally? Once located, you can select** resources applicable to your identified teaching objectives and refer to them in your planning.

- What computers are available? Will you have an electronic whiteboard, computers in the class, laptops or access to a suite of computers? In the first few days at school arrange a time with the IT co-ordinator to examine how the school manages its toolbox of software.
- Assess whether new resources need to be made in order to achieve the learning objective. Any new resources you create should be relevant and child friendly.
- Is a worksheet necessary? If so, when you create it make sure it allows children to demonstrate their understanding rather than just filling in boxes.
- If you need to use photocopied resources for your lesson find out the school's procedure for photocopying. Will administration staff or teaching assistants organise photocopying for teaching staff or is it the teacher's responsibility? If it is the latter, make time to understand how the photocopier works.
- Who will help to prepare and locate resources and create displays? If you have a certain amount of administrative or teaching assistant time you need to know how much and whom you should go to. You also need to identify areas for your displays with the teacher.
- Be organised. Ensure your resources are ready before the lesson. Photocopy any material in plenty of time. Photocopiers have a habit of jamming, usually just before an observed lesson, so have your copied resources ready well in advance. Collect any centrally stored resources, such as lenses for a science lesson, well beforehand. This will avoid a potentially stressful situation when you realise ten minutes before a lesson that they have disappeared from the science cupboard.

To teach a class of children on initial teaching practices can be a daunting process, so if you take steps to be planned and prepared you can focus on developing your classroom management style without the additional worry of lesson content.

REFLECTIVE TASK
REFLECTIVE TASK

When you have done your initial days in your placement setting you should ask yourself how well you can address Standard Q3b: 'Be aware of policies and practices of the workplace and share in collective responsibility for their implementation'.

Organise your notes under these headings:
- **school policies;**
- **the school day (routines);**
- **rules of behaviour;**
- **learning needs of the classes;**
- **resources.**

Review these notes at the end of your first week in school and ensure you have no gaps.

A SUMMARY OF **KEY POINTS**

> It is essential for you to spend a few days in school to gather information about the school and class.

> You may be placed with one year group but a number of other arrangements are possible, including sets, units and mixed age years.

> Find out about the school policies and read them early in your placement – all activity in school has to follow these policies.

> When you meet your class, create a professional, confident first impression.
> Learn school routines and staff habits. This will help you to feel at home.
> You should learn staff names and roles as soon as possible as you will be working with a number of people in school.
> In your first few days in school you should work out the class timetable and how you will fit in.

Resources

The government website **www.teachernet.gov.uk**. carries a huge range of supportive information for teachers. Use it to find out about the roles of staff in your school.

You should make sure you know the curriculum documentation relevant to your class and subjects. These can be found at: Qualifications and Curriculum Authority, 83 Piccadilly, London W1J 8QA. **www.qca.org.uk**. The source of information about the curriculum and assessment and also of the relevant documents.

Department of Education, Lifelong Learning and Skills (Wales), Welsh Assembly Government, Cathays Park, Cardiff CF10 3WQ. **www.old.accac.org.uk/eng.content.php?CID=5**. The source of information about the NC for Wales, which is also available online.

3
Learning to observe, plan and evaluate on teaching placement

By the end of this chapter you should know:

- **how to observe in a focused way;**
- **how medium-term, short-term and lesson plans are related;**
- **how to plan for parts of lessons and whole lessons;**
- **how to evaluate your lessons.**

When you have been in your placement school for a few days, whether it is your first or third placement, you will have collected a great deal of information and be ready to focus on the process of learning to teach successfully and meet the standards for QTS. Just as each school is different, each trainee is different. You will have a different background, different needs and so will require different experiences from your colleagues. The main techniques you will use to develop your teaching will be:

- **observation and discussion with teachers;**
- **planning;**
- **evaluating;**
- **teaching;**
- **assessing;**
- **completing school-based tasks.**

This chapter addresses observation, planning and evaluation.

Observation

Observation in your placement class(es) is particularly important because it is observation of what you are going to be doing very soon. The key thing to remember in all observations is that you are not observing to judge or criticise in a negative sense. You are observing to see:

- what children and teachers do in certain situations and with certain children;
- how certain actions and situations produce certain responses;
- how policies and theories work in practice;
- what you can learn from the situation.

The last point is the most important. You will not teach in the same way as anyone you watch but you will learn something from every lesson you observe. At the start of a placement there is something to be said for aping the teacher – or at least stepping into their shoes. The children in your class are used to certain routines and behaviours from their teacher, so you will appear authoritative and trustworthy to children if you know the routines and behave as they expect a teacher to behave.

The observation aspect of a placement is extremely important so do not rush through it. At the start of the placement you really need to observe everything – behaviour management, core subject teaching, assemblies, cross-curricular teaching, and staff meetings. Generally, you should observe a subject being taught before you teach it yourself. Some trainees overlook this in their enthusiasm to get going on the teaching part of the placement.

General observations

Early in a placement, you should do the following observations, making specific notes, then review your notes. These will enable you to make a start at teaching.

PRACTICAL TASK PRACTICAL TASK **PRACTICAL TASK** PRACTICAL TASK **PRACTICAL TASK**

Observing core subject lessons

Key Stage 1 and 2 – observe an English lesson and a maths lesson

Use the form below as a prompt to observe the lesson. Make notes (or use a sheet of a similar layout) about as much as you can so that you get an idea of the structure the teacher and children are used to, the key vocabulary, how arrangements are made for different children's needs and what the routines of the lessons are.

Prompt sheet for observing literacy and maths	
Lesson objective	Year .... No. of children ....
At the beginning of the lesson	
Teaching strategies	Class management and control
How does the teacher introduce the lesson objective? Does the teacher check prior knowledge, recall of previous material? How is the lesson set out to facilitate the start? Resources used? What do other adults in class do? Modelling of reading or writing? Mathematics games? Questioning? What is the balance of teacher-to-pupil talk? How long does this phase of the lesson last?	How does the teacher gain the children's attention and settle them? How does the teacher keep attention? What does the teacher do if a child is not paying attention? Evidence of pupils' interest and motivation?
During the lesson	
How do the pupils know what they will be doing? What sorts of tasks are they doing? Does the teacher work with one group or many? How do the other adults in the classroom work and with whom? Is there use of specific vocabulary? How are the pupils grouped? How are independent tasks related to the rest of the lesson? How long does this phase of the lesson last?	How does the teacher manage the transition from the mat (or group) to seat work? How do pupils get their resources? How does the teacher keep pupls on task? How does the teacher monitor the class? What 'rewards' does the teacher offer? (praise, eye contact, words, etc.) What sanctions does the teacher use? (frown, naming, etc.)
At the end of the lesson	
How does the teacher conclude the lesson? What learning does the teacher revisit? Which pupils report back on what they have done? How do pupils know how well they have done? How long does this phase of the lesson last? What do other adults in the class do? Is there homework? Is the next lesson referred to?	What is the signal for this phase of the lesson? How do pupils arrange their resources? How does the teacher manage the transition from seat work to the mat (or group)? Are pupils willing or enthusiastic to present their work? How does the teacher dismiss the class?

Early Years Foundation Stage – observe the teacher's role in a group session

Use one of the two forms below to observe a small group during one session. The first looks at one child activity, the second a whole session, involving more than one activity – possibly a practitioner-directed activity and a child-led activity. Observe as much as you can so that you get an idea of the routines the teacher and children are used to, the key vocabulary, how arrangements are made to include different children and what the learning objective of the session is.

Observing a practitioner working in an area of provision within the Early Years Foundation Stage	
• **Description of the area of provision (e.g. water/sand/role play area)** • **Information about the children involved (e.g. number, age, sex – is this a new activity for the children or one the children are very familiar with?)** • **Focus of the activity** • **What does the practitioner say and do?** • **What do the children say and do?** • **How does the practitioner monitor the children's achievements? How are children given feedback on their achievements?** • **Additional information, e.g. How long did the activity last? What did the children do next? What did the practitioner do next?**	• **Child interactions (non-verbal and verbal)** • **With self** • **With others** • **Actions including mark-making, drawing and any other recording included in the activity**

Prompt sheet for observing an early childhood setting session	
At the beginning of the lesson	
Entry to the session	
Adult activity	Child activity
How does the teacher welcome and direct the children? Are there routine 'beginning' processes, such as going to the mat, returning books, etc? How is the lesson set out to facilitate the start? Resources used? What do other adults in class do? What does the teacher or other group leader do to direct children? What does the teacher or other group leader do to engage children? Questioning? What does the teacher do if a child is not engaged in an activity? What is the balance of teacher-to-pupil talk? What area of learning do the activities address?	How does the child know what is available? Does the child choose the activity or is the child directed? How does the teacher attract attention? Evidence of pupil's interest and motivation? Does the child interact with other children? What vocabulary does the child use? What resources does the child use? Is there a produce, such as drawing, writing, model? What happens to this?
Self-selected activity	
How does the teacher welcome and direct the children? Are there routine 'beginning' processes, such as going to the mat, returning books, etc? How is the lesson set out to facilitate the start? Resources used? What do other adults in class do? What does the teacher or other group leader do to direct children? What does the teacher or other group leader do to engage children? Questioning? What does the teacher do if a child is not engaged in an activity? What is the balance of teacher-to-pupil talk? What area of learning do the activities address? How does the child know what is available? Does the child choose the activity or is the child directed?	How does the teacher attract attention? Evidence of pupil's interest and motivation? Does the child interact with other children? What vocabulary does the child use? What resources does the child use? Is there a produce, such as drawing, writing, model? What happens to this?
Session conclusion	
How does the teacher conclude the lesson? What learning does the teacher revisit? Which pupils report back on what they have done? What vocabulary do pupils use? How long does this phase of the lesson last? How does the teacher manage the transition from seat work to the mat (or group)?	What is the signal for this phase of the lesson? How do pupils arrange their resources? Are pupils willing or enthusiastic to recall activities? How does the teacher move the group on?

The other key issue you will be involved with is managing the behaviour of the children in your class. This is dealt with later, in much more detail. At the moment, however, the chief priority is to make a good start with this particular group of children. Read the school's behaviour policy as soon as you can and be sure you understand it. Make notes of the key points and check your observations to see what elements of the policy you have already seen in action. Ask your teacher, very early on, what she expects from the class, what rules she applies and what rewards and sanctions she offers. Most teachers are so used to this they may have to think to recall what they actually do but you need to know, so watch and ask. You should set the same standards, enforce the same rules and offer the same rewards as your teacher. To do this you must know what they are!

By the end of your preparation days in schools you should know most of the following.

- **What subjects and/or topics are being taught during your placement.**
- **The class routine.**
- **The names and broad characteristics of the children in your class, sets or groups.**
- **The school behaviour and health and safety policies and how these are implemented in your class.**
- **The names and roles of staff involved with your children.**
- **The daily routines of the class and school.**
- **Staffroom etiquette.**
- **The location and procedures for resources (in broad terms).**

You should be able to participate in lessons and talk confidently to the children.

Key Stages 1 and 2

For these key stages, you should make:

- **at least one observation of the teacher's behaviour management in a mathematics and an English lesson (see Chapter 8);**
- **at least one observation of the teacher's behaviour management in a foundation subject lesson (see Chapter 8);**
- **at least one observation of the teacher's behaviour management outside the classroom, the hall or the ICT suite (see Chapter 8);**
- **observations of mathematics, English and science lessons so that you can see the structures of these lessons (see Chapter 3);**
- **observations of break-time and lunchtime routines for the class.**

Early Years Foundation Stage

For this key stage, you should make:

- **at least one observation of the teacher's behaviour management in a teacher directed group session (see Chapter 8);**
- **at least one observation of the teacher's behaviour management in a child-led session (see Chapter 8);**
- **at least one observation of the teacher's behaviour management in the outdoor classroom (see Chapter 8);**
- **a focused observation of arrival and departure times and of the changeover time for part-time children – this not only introduces routines but also gives you models of how experienced staff interact with parents;**
- **focused observation of fruit or drinks times;**
- **focused observation of story or action rhyme times.**

MINI CASE MINI CASE MINI CASE **MINI CASE** MINI CASE MINI CASE **MINI CASE**

On my first placement I did some observation on my pre-placement serial days. I spent four days watching and helping groups. It meant I had seen most of a week and I had a feel for the rhythm of the class and expectations of behaviour. But I felt a bit of a fraud and I was really keen to get on to the teaching. I only had a four week placement, after all. I started teaching as soon as the placement began and built up to doing whole days in my second week. Looking back, I realise I didn't observe carefully enough at the beginning and now I wish I'd grabbed the opportunity when I had it. As the placement went on, I kept coming up with quite obvious questions about things like rules and routines that I should have been able to answer. I will be taking the observation part of the placement much more seriously on this placement.

Ann, PGCE

MINI CASE MINI CASE MINI CASE **MINI CASE** MINI CASE MINI CASE **MINI CASE**

As I had worked in the school for a year as a TA, I really didn't think I needed to do the observation tasks but my mentor was playing it by the book and made me use observation grids for lessons. It turned out to be really useful, particularly the observation for behaviour management. I found that when I took the class I was actually copying phrases and gestures the teacher used. I don't do that now, but it got me started and established me as a teacher. If I had to offer advice it would be to observe more than one teacher and see how different teachers implement the same policy.

Ellie, GTP

MINI CASE MINI CASE MINI CASE **MINI CASE** MINI CASE MINI CASE **MINI CASE**

My final placement was the really important one, because the way my course worked that was the assessed placement. I made sure I did the observations I needed. At the start of the placement I did routine observations of the teacher to learn how to manage the class. I also observed every subject before I taught it for the first time. As the placement progressed I used observations to address standards I still had outstanding. I did a really good afternoon observing the EAL teacher when she worked with some children in a group and some in a class. The strategies she used had been discussed in my course, but having the opportunity to see them used brought them alive and gave me ideas for using them in my class. It is hard to observe, because you feel you should be teaching but, as I see it, I might not get the chance when I am an NQT.

Jo, PGCE Early Years

Focused observations

As your placement progresses, you will be able to select your observations in a much more purposeful way. You might observe your teacher for the following reasons:

- **You have not had a chance to see a particular type of lesson. You will not want to wait three weeks before beginning your teaching and some subjects will be blocked so that they do not happen every week, or even every term.**
- **You have found a particular difficulty in your teaching and you want to find out how the teacher addresses this (and develop your own confidence). For example, if you are unsure about how to use your voice to gain children's attention or you need some strategies for teaching phonics.**

- **You have an outstanding target to address and observation is the best way of doing this. For instance, if you are aiming to improve your differentiation through questioning, first see how the teacher does it.**

To make the best possible use of these observations of your teacher's practice, make sure you have read any relevant documentation and are well prepared. If you are observing science, you will learn much more if you have read the school science policy and have looked at the relevant part of the Scheme of Work for science. If you have been able to see the planning for the lesson you will learn even more.

In your placement you will also observe and talk to other teachers in your school because they are a huge resource of expertise.

- **If you are in an Early Years setting you will observe the other members of the team, as the teaching of the group is a shared responsibility.**
- **If you do not have a chance to observe a particular type of teaching in your class your mentor can always arrange for you to go to another class. For instance, if your Key Stage 2 class are doing art but not D&T this term, you can go to another class to observe D&T.**
- **If another class has a particular resource you want to see in use, such as an interactive whiteboard (IWB), parachute or outdoor area, your mentor may help you arrange an observation.**
- **If another teacher in the school has a particular expertise your mentor may well arrange for you to observe them teaching in this area, for instance a leading English or mathematics teacher or an ICT co-ordinator.**
- **Observing a SENCO is very valuable because you can gain insight into the processes of the SEN code of practice and also see teaching strategies at work.**
- **Observing an EAL teacher or support assistant will not only help you to understand a wide range of strategies, it will also help you to include them in your teaching.**
- **Observing a class outside your key stages will help you to understand the experiences and needs of children in the key stages preceding and following yours. It will help you to think about the demands of transition.**

You need to be prepared to make the most of these observations. If you are going to observe the use of an IWB, review the notes of any training you have had so far. If you are going to talk to the SENCO and observe a group session, make sure you have read the school SEN policy and the IEPs of any children in your class.

Through observation you will learn that there are many different ways to be a successful teacher. On the basis of what you observe, you can start to develop a range of successful strategies. Once you use these strategies yourself they will become part of your personal teaching style.

Sample lesson observation format for Key Stages 1 and 2

The purpose of observing experienced teachers is to examine the range of techniques that the teacher is using in order to reflect on your own practice. You can use this grid to make notes.

Trainee's name	Teacher observed	Date and time
Class	Lesson topic	
Starting the lesson/transitions within the lesson	Links made to previous learning	
Teaching strategies	Pupil activities	
Organisation of the learning	Use of resources (including use of ICT)	
Management of pupils	Strategies for assessing pupil learning	
Consideration of special needs	Teacher presence in the classroom	
Summarising and extending the learning	Concluding the lesson	

Sample lesson observation format for Early Years Foundation Stage

Description of the area of provision (e.g. water/small world/role-play area)
Information about the children involved (e.g. number, age, sex – Is this a new activity for the children or one the children are very familiar with?)
Focus of the activity – EYFS

What does the practitioner say and do?	What do the children say and do?

How does the practitioner monitor the children's achievements? How are children given feedback on their achievements?
Additional information, e.g. How long did the activity last? What did the children do next? What did the practitioner do next?

Planning and differentiation

There is no such thing as a good teacher who cannot plan well. Planning is the basis of good teaching and you have a number of reasons for becoming good at planning. First of all, you have to demonstrate that you meet the standards for QTS.

- **Section 3, Professional Skills, requires you to meet Standards Q22, 23 and 24 for planning.**
- **Q22 Plan for progression across the age and ability range for which you are trained, designing effective learning sequences within lessons and across series of lessons and demonstrating secure subject knowledge.**
- **Q23 Design opportunities for learners to develop their literacy, numeracy and ICT skills.**

- **Q24** Plan homework or other out-of-class work to sustain learners' progress and to extend and consolidate their learning.
- **Q25** (b) build on prior knowledge, (c) adapt their language to suit the learners they teach, introducing new ideas and cpncepts clearly and using explanations, questions, discussion. (d) manage the learning of indidiiduals, groups and whole classes, modifying their teaching to suit the stage of the lesson.
- **Q33** Ensure that colleagues working with them are appropriately involved in supporting learners and understand the roles they are expected to fulfil.

To demonstrate these standards you will build your expertise at planning gradually as you progress through your placements.

The theory of planning is relatively straightforward and by the time you arrive for your placement you should know about some of the factors shaping the choice of what children learn and how they learn it.

Every Child Matters and National Curriculum
Early Years Foundation Stage
(Key Stages 1 and 2 English, mathematics, science, ICT, PE, history,
geography, DT, art as well as PSHE, citizenship and RE),

Primary Framework for Literacy and Mathematics and schemes of work for foundation subjects

Local Authority guidance and policies

School policies and school targets

Medium-term planning and class targets

Each child's individual needs on the basis of previous assessments and individual education targets
(IEPs)

Weekly planning

Previous lesson or daily planning

Your lesson

- The rights of children and young people as set out in *Every Child Matters* (Green Paper) and the Children Act 2004, in relation to:
  - physical and mental health and emotional well-being;
  - protection from harm and neglect;
  - education, training and recreation;
  - the contribution by them to society;
  - social and economic well-being.
- The National Curriculum and personal, social and health education (PSHE) and citizenship requirements. Together with the RE curriculum these provide much of the content of our curriculum at Key Stages 1 and 2. At Key Stages 1 and 2 the National Primary Strategy Framework for teaching literacy and mathematics and Schemes of work give advice about teaching, but are not statutory.

- In Early Years Foundation Stage the Early Learning Goals and six areas of learning stand in the place of a curriculum. This statutory curriculum is supplemented at Early Years Foundation Stage through the curriculum guidance for the Early Years Foundation Stage.
- Local authorities will offer guidance about teaching and have requirements and policies for the curriculum. These and the school's policies and targets will also shape the material planned for lessons.
- Within school the curriculum co-ordinators will monitor plans and ensure the curriculum is addressed progressively and continuously

You need to be involved in different levels of planning during your training. You will have to demonstrate that you know about medium-term planning, especially for English, mathematics, science and ICT at Key Stages 1 and 2, or all six areas of learning for Early Years Foundation Stage.

Medium-term planning

Drawing up a medium-term plan for, say, a half term, means dividing up the learning for the half term so that it can be taught in a continuous, progressive way that meets the needs of all the learners in the class. This is not as simple as it sounds. To do it you need:

- good knowledge of the curriculum documents (NC, Primary Framework for the teaching of literacy and mathematics, EYFS, etc.);
- good subject knowledge so that you can make sensible divisions and links between elements of knowledge and skill;
- an understanding of how you will teach the subjects and what the pupils' likely responses will be;
- some experience or knowledge of how long it will take for children to learn each element of your plan.

These require some experience, so medium-term planning is usually the first type of planning you see but the last type of planning you actually do.

You may find it difficult to obtain experience of medium-term planning on your placements because teachers in school do this sort of planning well in advance and often refer to last year's plans. Also teachers may not work individually on medium-term planning but do it in planning teams involving all the teachers teaching the same year group or key stage. It is quite usual for curriculum co-ordinators to work with planning teams or check their plans for a particular subject to ensure that the curriculum for that subject is covered effectively.

Medium-term plans are usually expressed in terms of broad objectives for what the children should learn and these are specifically referenced to (or copied from) the National Curriculum programmes of study, schemes of work for EYFS subjects, guidance on RE, PSHE and citizenship and strategies to address the Early Years Foundation Stage curriculum. To demonstrate that you know about medium-term planning you should meet with your teacher specifically to discuss planning using the guidance suggested in the practical task below. You can see exemplar medium-term plans for English or mathematics on the standards site (www.standards.dfes.gov.uk). If you have the opportunity to attend a medium-term planning meeting, even if it is not for a term when you will be on placement, you should seize the chance as it will give you the best possible training. This is an opportunity your mentor may be able to arrange for you.

Weekly or unit planning

A weekly plan, or plan for a sequence of lessons over a longer period, is constructed from the medium-term plan. It is more specific than a medium-term plan and will include not only the learning objectives but also the teaching activities, resources and assessment points of the lessons in the sequence. Teachers will usually have a weekly plan for each subject at Key Stages 1 and 2, although there will often be strong links across the curriculum.

In the Early Years Foundation Stage the plan for a week, or unit of work, will usually be written by at least the teacher and teaching assistant. It may involve a larger team. It will address all the areas of development and will usually be planned around a theme such as summer, the seaside, diwali, growing, myself, etc. This is to emphasise the links between different areas of development and ensure the learning makes sense to very young children.

There is no one correct format for weekly or unit plans. Most schools have at least one set format that they use for planning but many have different formats for different key stages or even different formats for different subjects. This is especially true in the case of literacy and mathematics at Key Stages 1 and 2, where the structures of the lessons may demand different planning grids. Weekly plans will be referenced to the relevant curriculum documents and will break down learning and teaching so that children can achieve the learning objectives. This is a difficult skill because, as well as everything necessary for medium-term planning, you need to know:

- **what children have already done, know and can do;**
- **the likely response of children to what you are planning;**
- **the pace at which children can work;**
- **any individual needs that demand differentiation at a weekly planning level.**

You may find it easiest to use the interactive planning tool for literacy and mathematics available at **www.standards.dfes.gov.uk/primaryframework/planningtool**

Example forms for planning a sequence of lessons

Experienced teachers in some schools will teach from their weekly or unit plans. At the start of each placement you will not be able, or ready, to do this but you will use the teacher's weekly plans right from the start as guidance so that you know what to expect from lessons or sessions you are observing. By looking at weekly plans you can at least be sure what the learning objective of the lesson is and how you should support children in achieving it. When you start teaching you will plan your early lessons and parts of lessons on the basis of the teacher's weekly plans.

As your placement progresses, you will be required to write weekly plans (or sequences of lesson plans) for core subjects if you are a Primary trainee or across the six areas of learning in the Early Years Foundation Stage curriculum if you are an Early Years trainee. This does not mean that you will have to do this unsupported. You will seek careful advice about your first weekly plan and use the teacher's medium-term plans as a basis for writing weekly plans. If weekly planning is done as a year group, setting or phase team activity you will be able to do your weekly planning this way but you will be expected to make a significant contribution and to lead the planning at this level before you can achieve the Standards for QTS.

Sequence of lessons **Term/Year** **Teaching group**

(This derives from the school's medium-term plans)

Curriculum subject/Theme/Area(s) of learning					
Broad learning objectives Specific references to Early Learning Goals, NC, PNF for Literacy or Mathematics, Agreed Syllabus for RE	**Focused learning objectives** Attitudes, skills, knowledge and understanding	**Key activities**	**Resources**	**Cross-curricular aspects**	**Planned method of assessment**
Broad learning objectives	**Learning objectives** stating anticipated achievement in one or more of the following: • attitudes (show...) • skills (be able to...) • knowledge (know that...) • understanding (develop concept of...) These form the basis of assessment and are judged through planned outcomes.	**Activities** should: • enable learning objectives to be met • include a variety of experiences that progressively develop children's learning • recognise pupils' diverse needs. (including pupils with SEN, gifted and talented pupils, and pupils with EAL) • take account of pupils' gender and ethnicity	**Resources** should be: • influenced by learning objectives • listed in detail • considered with health and safety in mind • related to displays where relevant	**Opportunities** to develop significant and planned attitudes, skills, knowledge and understanding across the curriculum in (e.g.): • English • ICT • PSHE/Citizenship • other NC subjects/ areas of learning where significant	**Anticipated evidence** • to demonstrate achievement of learning objectives, and to inform assessment and record keeping. (may be observational, verbal, written or graphic evidence, depending on activity) • to reflect a range of assessment methods

Sequence of lessons **Term/Year** **Teaching group**

(This derives from the school's medium-term plans)

Curriculum subject/Theme/Area(s) of learning

Broad learning objectives	Focused learning objectives	Key activities	Resources	Cross-curricular aspects	Planned method of assessment
Broad learning objectives	Learning objectives	Activities	Resources	Opportunities	Anticipated evidence

PRACTICAL TASK PRACTICAL TASK PRACTICAL TASK PRACTICAL TASK PRACTICAL TASK

Obtain your teacher's medium-term plans as soon as possible (usually on placement preparation days). Examine them carefully and ensure you know the following:

- **What period of time does each part of the plan cover? What period of time does the plan cover in total?**
- **For Key Stages 1 or 2 what parts of the National Curriculum, Primary Framework for Literacy and Mathematics, Schemes of work for the foundation subjects, PSHE curriculum, citizenship guidance and RE syllabus does this medium-term plan address? Make sure you look up all these elements and read them in detail because you do need to demonstrate familiarity with these documents.**
- **For Early Years Foundation Stage, what literacy and mathematics outcomes and areas of learning and development does this medium-term plan address? Make sure you look up all these elements and read them in detail because you do need to demonstrate familiarity with these documents.**

This part of the task will take you at least an hour or so and should be done before you go on to the weekly plan.

Ask your teacher for his or her weekly plans for one of the weeks included in the medium-term plan. Ensure you can answer the following:

- **Which parts of the medium-term plan does the weekly plan address?**
- **Which parts of the relevant curriculum documents does this refer to? (You will be able to see this if you have done the first part of the task well.)**
- **How long will each lesson or session in the weekly plan be?**
- **What additional detail does a weekly plan contain that a medium-term plan does not?**

If you are on placement in Key Stages 1 or 2, you can now focus on one part of the weekly plan, perhaps mathematics, or science. If you are in Early Years Foundation Stage you need to look at all the areas of learning.

- **What resources are needed for the lessons in the weekly plan?**
- **Who will be teaching the lessons in the weekly plan? Are they for a particular set or area of learning?**

Discuss your chosen element of weekly planning with your teacher. You should ask:

- **How do you derive a weekly plan from the medium-term plan?**
- **What do you do if the children do not make the predicted learning gains in one week?**
- **How do you ensure that the learning is accessible to all the children in the class?**
- **How do you differentiate for children who have SEN, EAL or are in the gifted and talented register?**
- **Please can you show me how you include children with IEPs or targets?**

Lesson or session planning

A lesson or session plan is written from a weekly (or longer-term) plan. It is a detailed document that addresses every element of the lesson/session. For you this has two main purposes.

First, a lesson plans enables you to demonstrate that you can select the appropriate objectives, teaching methods, assessment points and resources to teach an interesting, relevant and successful lesson. Lesson plans serve to show you can identify children's learning and to lead on to the next teaching experience. Secondly, writing lesson plans is a formative experience that gives you the chance to rehearse lessons before you do them. In this way you learn to deliver the content you mean to deliver. You also learn to manage challenging aspects of teaching such as pace, questioning, class management and enthusiasm. By planning lessons carefully in writing, you will gradually develop the mental scripts for teaching, assessment and class management that experienced teachers have so that, eventually, you no longer need to write lesson plans. At the beginning of every placement you will be expected to write lesson/session plans for every lesson or session you teach but later in the placement your mentor may suggest you no longer need to do this. If this happens you may teach from weekly plans.

There is no perfect lesson plan format but lesson plans need to include most of the following.

- **Class/group taught.**
- **Time and duration of lesson.**
- **Learning objective(s). This is the most important point on the plan. What do you want the children to learn, understand or do as a result of your lesson? Think very carefully about expressing lesson objectives so that they are reasonable and achievable. A single session or lesson may address or contribute to a literacy or mathematics objective or to an EYFS area of learning but no lesson will cover one of these big objectives. You may want to reference them on your lesson plan but phrase your lesson objective accurately so that the children can achieve it.**
- **Reference to the relevant curriculum documentation (NC, FTLM, EYFS, schemes of work, etc.).**
- **The structure of the session. Does the lesson have a three-part structure? Most lessons have an introduction, main body and a plenary. A mathematics lesson might have a mental/oral starter, a main activity and a plenary. An English lesson might have a shared part, a main activity and a plenary. In Early Years Foundation Stage is there a teacher-led then child-selected activity? Do nursery children do a plan/do/review format?**
- **The timings of each part of the lesson.**
- **Key vocabulary to be used.**
- **Key questions to be asked.**
- **Key teaching points.**
- **Role of the teacher and teaching assistants.**
- **Learning activity (what the children do).**
- **List of resources and use of outdoor classroom (for Early Years Foundation Stage).**
- **Identified outcomes (how will you assess whether the children have achieved their learning objective?).**
- **Note of pupils' previous experience.**
- **Cross-curricular links.**
- **Use of ICT.**
- **Identified health and safety issues (such as glue guns, the need to wear coats, etc.).**
- **An evaluation section.**

Here are some examples of lesson plans and formats. No format is perfect but any of these can be adapted and changed. Your course tutor or mentor will probably suggest a format you might use. Your mentor will certainly, at some point in the placement, suggest that you adapt your lesson plan format to help you address a particular target. For example:

- **If you are finding it difficult to maintain the pace of a lesson, you may want to plan in five minute intervals and note down the times at the side of our lesson plans.**
- **If you are having difficulty focusing on key vocabulary, you may want to highlight or embolden this in your plan.**
- **If preparation is a particular target, you may need to list resources especially carefully.**
- **If moving the children around the classroom is an issue for you, you may want to plan transitions very carefully.**

Your lesson plans could well change format for a short time to assist you in addressing your target.

Generic lesson plan to adapt for specific subjects (Key Stages 1 and 2)

Date	Class/year group or set including number of pupils
Pupils' previous experience	
Notes from previous lesson including errors and misconceptions that need to addressed in this lesson	
FTLM/NC references including, where appropriate, level descriptors and/or relationship with QCA schemes of work and the school's scheme of work	Learning objectives
Cross-curricular focus: spiritual, social, cultural, moral	
QTS Standards for observation	
Resources for each phase of the lesson	Subject-specific language

Specific expectations for behaviour (make clear to pupils)			

Appropriate speaking and listening objectives. Planned links, where appropriate, to English, mathematics and ICT for all subjects.

Mental/oral starter/shared reading or writing or other introductory activity (Time)

Assessment

Activity and questions to ask   Can the pupils?

Introduction to the main activity (Time)	
Teacher	Pupils

Main activity (Time) Phase	Low attainers	Middle attainers	High attainers
Assessment Can the pupils?	Extension/challenge	Extension/challenge	Extension/challenge

Teacher's role during the main activity	
Differentiation/target-setting including IEPs where appropriate	Use of in-class support, including guidance to supporting adult(s)
Plenary (Time) Key questions to ask/areas to discuss Introduce homework where appropriate Note any errors/misconceptions to focus on in the next lesson on this area.	
Evaluation of the lesson	
Annotate the plan, using a different colour. Add other working notes here. After the session make any relevant notes that will help you to support pupils' progression/plan a similar session. This may include references to specific pupils (which may or may not need to go on their records)/ideas to reinforce the learning/suggestions for alternative organisational strategies/comments on the appropriateness of the resources.	
Focus on pupils' learning	
Pupils not reaching the objectives, how and why?	Pupils exceeding reaching the objectives, how and why?
Notes for next lesson focusing on teaching	
Good aspects of teaching	Areas for development

Generic lesson plan to adapt for Early Years Foundation Stage areas of learning

Focus of the activity	
Children involved (e.g. number, age, sex – Is this a new activity for the children or one the children are very familiar with?) Self-selection? Practitioner-directed?	
Resources/Description of the area of provision (e.g. water/small world/role-play area)	
Key practitioner vocabulary and questions?	What do the children say and do?
Evidence of achievement	Interaction with others?
Observations of participants	Action for future activity

Your very first plans

Your very first plans on a placement will probably not be for whole lessons or sessions. Initially, you will plan for short parts of lessons or sessions such as the mental/oral starter in a mathematics lesson, a guided reading session for a small group of children, supervision of an outdoor activity or a whole class phonics game. In planning these parts of lessons you will have the chance to pay attention to detail and really concentrate on some important aspects of using plans such as:

- **ensuring you say what you plan to say;**
- **maintaining a pace that is brisk and engaging but not so fast that the children are lost;**
- **questioning and interactive teaching.**

Planning parts of lessons and teaching them is a good start to building up responsibility for whole lessons. Initially, you will want to ask your teacher to look at your plans and make suggestions. In this way you are more likely to pitch the activity at the right level for the children. This is a skilled exercise that demands some experience of the children and their previous work. When going into a new class you will need the support of the class teacher to pitch the level of the activities right.

Planner for a mental/oral starter

Date		Group/class		
Duration		Framework for teaching literacy and mathematics reference		
Resources		Mathematical, literacy, etc., language		
Activity				
Questions				
Less confident		Confident		More confident
Assessment				
Less confident		Confident		More confident
Evaluation				

Planning for other adults in the class or setting

As your placement progresses, you will develop expertise and speed in your planning. You will plan for a wider range of subjects and a wider range of situations. One key issue you need to consider, as you assume a greater role in planning for the class and as soon as you are planning whole class lessons, is planning for teaching assistants. It is usual for teachers to teach with teaching assistants and to plan for them.

A planning format for a teaching assistant

Date.................................... Lesson focus...

Activity (a brief account of the activity and the TA's role in any whole class introduction, shared reading, mental and oral, etc.)
Equipment needed
Key vocabulary to use
Key questions to use

Objectives
1
2
3

For completion by the TA after group work

Names		can do	needs help	notes
	1			
	2			
	3			
	1			
	2			
	3			
	1			
	2			
	3			
	1			
	2			
	3			
	1			
	2			
	3			

In the Early Years Foundation nursery practitioners will probably use the same planning sheets as the teacher and will make evaluations and assessments like the teacher. In Key Stages 1 and 2 there is a wider variety of practice. To ensure you work well with the teaching assistant, we suggest you use a set format to present clear expectations of what you would like the teaching assistant to do. You should also leave a space for the TA to write assessment notes about how well the children achieved the objective. These notes may well affect your future planning.

Frequently asked questions

1 'I have been planning my lessons on the computer every night. It is taking me hours and hours to type them up and I am becoming very tired. What can I do?'

Your priority is clear, accessible, useful plans and it does not matter whether they are written or word processed. If writing by hand works better for you, then write the plans by hand. If it worries you, you can always word process plans for the sessions when your mentor or course tutor is observing you. This has the added bonus of showing that you are making an effort to assist the observer and you will gain points for taking a professional approach. Of course, you may find that the computer is faster if you are adapting Internet plans or using the planning tool for the Framework for teaching literacy and mathematics.

2 'I have found loads of plans on the internet but my teacher says I can't just print these off and use them. Why not?'

There are hundreds of lesson plans available on sites like the Standards site (DfES), the Hamilton Trust site, the Primary Strategy site, etc. There is nothing wrong with these plans except that they are not necessarily right for your situation. To use them you must adapt them to the needs and prior experience of your children as well as the weekly or medium-term planning for your class. Once a unit of work is started, each group of children will work through at a different rate and no plans created at a distance can accommodate this. If you can adapt plans from the internet to meet the needs of your children and the pace of your planning, they may work very well for you. Most trainees use adapted, internet-based plans some of the time but many say they find it is just as quick to start from scratch. However, you cannot have too many ideas and Internet plans are ideal for generating ideas.

3 'I am on placement in an Early Years Foundation Stage unit and the staff are used to planning together as a team on a weekly basis. Each member of staff plans one or two areas of the curriculum. How can I get involved and get the right experience?'

This is a common situation and your mentor will have ways to involve you. You might start by creating more detailed session plans from the team's weekly plans for each area of learning you work in. This will help you to focus on the details of sessions such as key language, interaction with children and observation. As the placement progresses you will take a larger role in planning meetings and by the end of your placement you should be able to make helpful suggestions towards the weekly plan. Remember to do (and plan) the routine aspects of teaching at Early Years Foundation Stage that the team may not plan. These include reading to children regularly, managing fruit time, helping children to change books and take home books and story sacks, managing the home time routine and welcome, and modelling writing. Plan these sessions carefully.

4 'I write my lesson plans out in proper sentences but my friend uses note form. Who is right?'

Probably both of you. If note form is quicker and still includes detail it is a good working compromise. You can write in more detail when you know the lesson plan will be the object of scrutiny, such as for an observation by your mentor.

5 'I have planned and taught lessons for English, mathematics, ICT and science (and other subjects) and now my mentor is asking me to do sequences of lessons. She insists I should do sequences in the core subjects but I'd rather do sequences in art and music. Can she insist?'

Yes – she has your training interests at heart. To meet the professional standards for the award of QTS you must demonstrate you can plan lessons and sequences of lessons in the core subjects and ICT. A different level of planning is required for planning across the foundation subjects at Key Stages 1 and 2. You must be able to plan foundation subject lessons from the teacher's medium-term plans, with teacher support, in five core subjects. This is a rather less demanding level of planning. Your mentor is making sure you use your ITT time to focus on the planning that will enable you to meet the standards.

6 'In my last mentor observation the mentor said the objectives on my lesson plan were inappropriate. I used a Primary Framework for Teaching literacy outcome. What have I done wrong?'

Well done for referring to the PFTL objectives. This shows you are using documents to address Standard Q15. However, the PFTL objectives are designed to be used for planning at a higher level – over a number of sessions. For example, the Y4 objective 'Use setting and characterisation to engage readers' interest' would be fine for a weekly or unit plan, but for a lesson, the objective might be 'To write a character description of a "good" character', or 'To write a character description, selecting vocabulary to make the character interesting'.

Evaluation

Planning goes hand in hand with evaluation. To demonstrate Standard Q7(a) you need to be able to improve your performance through self-evaluation. This is discussed in more detail in the next chapter but cannot go unmentioned here. Evaluation means considering:

- **how well the children achieved your objectives;**
- **how well you planned, taught and managed teaching in relation to your targets.**

You will be required to include evaluations on most of your lesson plans and you will see spaces for these in the proformas above. Evaluations will usually be brief and will usually focus on two aspects: what you did and what the children learned.

If every time you taught a lesson you wrote a detailed critique of your performance as a teacher, linked to the standards, you would never have time to teach. Perhaps this is why some trainees start every evaluation they write with the dreaded sentence 'The lesson went well'. This is an ineffective evaluation because it tells the reader nothing except that the trainee survived to teach again. What went well? Does 'well' mean the children learned something?

It is much more useful to focus on particular aspects of your teaching to evaluate and improve. This is the role of the targets that are discussed in later chapters. For example, if you are really concentrating on managing the class, then you need to monitor how successful you are at managing behaviour, what strategies worked and what progress you are making. If you have this sort of evaluation for a series of lessons you can decide when you have achieved this target and when it is time to identify a new target.

When you begin planning and teaching you will probably be very keen to hear positive evaluations but less keen to hear advice on improvement. However, you should develop your ability to listen to advice and act on it. Your teacher will be in a good position to obtain a wide ranging view of your performance and will help you to evaluate in a critical but positive way.

When your evaluation comment identifies work to be done always say what you propose to do in response. The very best planning is the sort that clearly uses evidence from children's previous attainment and leads on to influence the planning and teaching of the next session or lesson. This sort of evidence may be the annotations to a lesson plan you make in response to previous evaluations.

Differentiation

In order to meet the diverse learning needs of pupils, teachers aim to teach the knowledge, skills and understanding in ways that suit their pupils' abilities – this is called differentiation. You demonstrate your ability to do this through your professional knowledge (Q10), planning (Q22), and your teaching (Q25a, b, c and especially d). When planning, teachers should set high expectations and provide opportunities for all children to achieve including:

- **boys and girls;**
- **children with special educational needs;**
- **children with disabilities;**
- **children from all social and cultural backgrounds;**
- **children of different ethnic groups including travellers, refugees and asylum seekers;**
- **children from diverse linguistic backgrounds.**

Differentiation is represented in different forms in your planning, and involves:

- **Presentation – planning to use a variety of media to present ideas, offering vocabulary or extra diagrams to those who need more support. Writing grids might be a form of presentation to help young writers who need extra support, where more confident writers do not have such support.**
- **Content – selecting appropriately so that there is content that suits most children with additional content available to some. This might mean some children completing six calculations where others complete ten.**
- **Resources – use resources that support pupils' needs such as writing frame, language master word banks or spellmaster machines for poor spellers. For children with EAL you might need to ensure that target vocabulary is available in a written form.**
- **Grouping – grouping pupils of similar ability for targeted support or pairing with a more able pupil, teaching assistant or language support teacher.**
- **Task – matching tasks to pupils' abilities. This can mean different tasks for different pupils. It is sometimes a good idea to offer different tasks that address the same objectives to different pupils so that they can achieve success.**
- **Support – offering additional adult or peer assistance, from a TA, language support teacher or more**

experienced child.

- **Time – giving more or less time to complete a given task can make the task more suitable to the particular pupils.**

As you develop your planning you will need to be sure to address the needs of all children. To do this you will plan different activities, support, resources, content, time and presentation so that all the children can achieve the learning objectives. Although this sounds simple it demands really good knowledge of the content, the children and a range of teaching strategies. At first you may well over- or underestimate what children know and can do. You will only achieve appropriate differentiation by working closely with the teacher so that you find out what strategies are available and which work for these children. Key resources will be TAs, language support staff and the IEPs written for children with special needs. All these should be planned into your lessons.

REFLECTIVE TASK
REFLECTIVE TASK

Review your early plans for:

- **a whole class session;**
- **a group activity;**
- **an individual task to be used with a larger group or class of children.**

Focus on your use of questioning in each of these situations.

How have you differentiated the task to meet the needs of individuals?

Ensure you have considered:

- **who you will question;**
- **the function of the questions (bringing to mind knowledge, checking, keeping order, etc.);**
- **how you will phrase questions and what key vocabulary you will use;**
- **what sorts of answers you are looking for.**

Questioning is a key area for differentiation.

A SUMMARY OF **KEY POINTS**

> **Observation is the first step towards teaching. You will need to observe at the start of a placement and during the placement. Do not teach a subject you have not observed. Observation is also a tool for increasing your knowledge and experience. Choose your observations to meet your training needs.**

> **Planning is the foundation of good teaching and learning. Careful planning will help you to teach the right content, manage the class, maintain a good pace, give children feedback and assess learning.**

> **You will encounter medium-term planning for a half term, weekly planning and short-term, lesson or session planning.**

> **Begin planning small elements of sessions and build up to whole sessions. When you can plan lessons build up to sequences of lessons or core subject lessons.**

> Planning is often done in teams. You will be planning with the support of your teacher and, possibly, a wider teaching team.

> Seize any opportunity to be involved in medium-term planning and to attend planning meetings.

> Differentiate your plans so that all children are included and plan for teaching assistants and other practitioners.

> Evaluation is your tool for ensuring learning takes place – in yourself and the children. Evaluate lessons and sequences of lessons.

Resources

The Primary Frameworks for Teaching Literacy and Mathematics (PFTLM) are at **www.standards.dfes.gov.uk/primaryframeworks.**

The TDA has an ITT professional resource network that addresses many aspects of multicultural and multilingual education: **www.multiverse.ac.uk.**

The teacher support network **www.teachernet.gov.uk** has additional advice about planning and offers access to over 2000 lesson plans.

4
Learning to teach on placement

By the end of this chapter you should:

- **know how to build up your teaching on placement;**
- **know some of the features of interactive teaching;**
- **know how to set homework;**
- **recognise opportunities to play a wider role in school;**
- **understand the role of school-based tasks in building up your experience.**

Teaching

Surprisingly, many trainees find teaching a class or group is less challenging than planning and assessing. You can aim to demonstrate that you meet standards in all three sections:

In Professional Attributes, you:

Q1   Have high expectations of children ... including a commitment to ensuring they achieve their full educational potential.

Q4   Communicate effectively with children.

In Professional Knowledge you:

Q10   Have knowledge and understanding of a range of teaching, learning and behaviour management strategies and know how to adapt them, personalise learning and provide opportunities for learners to achieve their potential.

Q14   Have a secure knowledge of their subjects/curricular areas and related pedagogy to enable them to teach effectively.

Q15   Know the relevant statutory and non-statutory curricula.

In Professional Skills, you:

Q25   Teach lessons and sequences of lessons which
      (a) use a range of teaching strategies and resources
      (b) build on prior knowledge
      (c) use language to suit learners, introduce ideas and concepts clearly, use explanations, questions, discussions and plenaries effectively.

To tackle this daunting list of standards you should aim to build up your teaching gradually. Start by planning and teaching small parts of lessons, based on the class teacher's plans and using strategies you have seen the teacher using. This might mean you start in an L7 Foundation Key Stage class by planning and managing a small word activity or a dramatic play area and work to interact effectively with children who choose to do that activity. In a Key Stage 1 class you might start out by doing a whole class mental/oral starter in mathematics or a shared reading session in English. In Key Stage 2 you might start by taking a group guided reading session or using the interactive whiteboard to introduce a whole-class main activity in mathematics or literacy.

You will move on to teaching complete lessons with the support of the teacher, who will help you to establish yourself as a teacher, to maintain a purposeful working environment and to teach the appropriate material. As you develop confidence, a suitable relationship with the children and a range of strategies for teaching, you will plan and teach a wide range of lessons or sessions, increasing the range of strategies for differentiation and ensuring all the children's needs are met. Eventually, you will plan and teach sequences of lessons that take the children through a process of learning about a topic or set of skills. This process of building up your level of responsibility and range of teaching techniques is different for each trainee because your experience is unique and each class of children is different. We asked seven NQTs for their top ten tips for beginner teachers and this is what they suggested:

Know what you are talking about

You must be absolutely clear about what you are teaching so that you can introduce the topic clearly to the children and understand and address their errors and misconceptions. No one else can do this for you and if you do not have the necessary subject knowledge you may teach the wrong content or be unable to help children. Always research your lessons so that you can demonstrate Standard Q14 and check the relevant curriculum documentation.

Prepare your resources well in advance

If you do not do this, something is bound to come up. As a trainee teacher it will be harder for you to locate resources or have them produced, because you do not know the system. If you leave organising your resources until just before a session things are certain to go wrong (the copier will jam, the cornflour will go missing or there will be no blue paint). You will become flustered and this will unsettle the children.

Put up your objectives and discuss them

If you just write up objectives for Key Stages 1 and 2 children, the objectives will become so much classroom wallpaper. If you just discuss objectives, some children will forget them. If you write them up, hold them up and discuss what they mean, there is a good chance that both you and the children will understand them.

Explain very clearly

Explain then check whether the children have understood you. Every teacher will be able to tell you about times when they have not said what they meant and have been faced with baffled children. Most children will answer 'yes' to the question 'Do you understand what you have to do?' so avoid this question. Say: 'Tell me what you are going to do'. Occasionally, you will find that they do not know and this will usually be because you have missed out a vital point. Try using little cards with key words to remind yourself of the points you have to explain.

Act as if you know the rules, rewards and sanctions

This will give you confidence: if you act as if you do not know the rules you will lose credibility in the eyes of your class. Even the youngest Early Years Foundation Stage child can spot someone who does not know what they are doing. If you are unsure, you can always ask a child but ask in a way that suggests confidence: 'Right, now show me where you keep your book. Well done!' is better than giving an indication that you do not know what to do.

Keep children moving and keep them involved

If your questioning involves a whole range of children and demands that they do something in response to questions, they are much more likely to engage with the activity. In the section on questioning (see page 64) there is more advice on this. Even a little movement can make an activity more memorable and purposeful for children. For instance, ask children to perform action rhymes, not just recite them. Get them to stand up and sit down as they answer a rapid-fire tables test. These are small, important things but they can have a surprisingly positive effect.

Keep up the pace

Pace the lesson so that you maintain the children's engagement and fit your plenary in. The plenary is a very important part of a session. Your can restate the teaching points, monitor who has understood and take the learning forward in a very brief plenary. Even at Early Years Foundation Stage children learn from a brief reflection. Maintaining pace is a real challenge when you begin teaching.

Ham it up

Use your voice, body and other visual aids in an exaggerated way to generate enthusiasm, interest and motivation.

Get to know the children and their abilities quickly

This is a counsel of perfection and you will find it very challenging. However, the sooner you have a broad understanding of children's current abilities and past experience, the sooner your lessons will go smoothly. Most teachers and trainees experience, working with a new class, lessons that turn out to be unexpectedly short or long. Until you know the class you are not able to match the work to the children's needs. Meanwhile, check with your teacher often and get him or her to check lesson plans.

Give prompt, balanced feedback

Whether this is about knowledge, skills or behaviour, the most important thing is that you notice and respond. Generally, a small, positive response such as a nod, smile or 'Well done' is all that is required. Do not praise effusively – this devalues the currency. Remember that the children who need the feedback most are often those who are least able to wait for it.

Do not panic – ever

You are in control for as long as you stay calm and are enjoying your work. If you panic you will lose control and find yourself acting unwisely.

Questioning and interactive teaching

Questioning and interactive teaching are vital aspects of Early Years or Primary teaching. You must demonstrate that you can:

Q25(c)   adapt language to suit the learners you teach, introducing new ideas and concepts clearly and use explanations, questions, discussions and plenaries effectively.

Interactive teaching involves a powerful set of strategies to ensure children learn in ways that suit them best. It is also a very powerful ally for behaviour management. Children who are interested, involved and engaged with an activity are easy to manage.

Questioning

Optimise the interaction between you and your pupils by ensuring that your questioning is as effective as possible. Questioning, either by the teacher or among the children, is a crucial part of introducing a topic and effective at the end of the lesson. It allows you to

- **identify what children already know;**
- **engage them in finding out more;**
- **explore misconceptions and errors;**
- **theorise aloud about new ideas;**
- **demonstrate new learning.**

There are a number of types of questions:

- *closed* **questions have one clear answer (e.g. 'How much is two add one?');**
- *open* **questions have open-ended answers (e.g. 'How does the cornflour feel?');**
- *product* **questions are designed to find the answer to a particular problem;**
- *process* **questions are meant to elicit procedures, processes and rules used to get the answers.**

The mix of question types you use will depend on the objectives of the session. Your teaching is likely to be more effective if you use more open than closed questions, and more process than product questions. It is very easy to maintain a brisk pace with low-level closed questions but this does not ensure the best learning.

How long you wait for answers depends on the type of question asked. Allow three seconds or so for a lower level factual recall question, and 10–15 seconds for higher level questions (those requiring more sophisticated thinking skills). This will seem a very long wait indeed, but avoid the temptation to fill the space with talk. After the waiting time has passed you should prompt the children. If you ask a complex question requiring a lot of thought, allow children some time to work the answer out on their own – this is where talk partners or the use of small whiteboards are invaluable. You will sometimes want to ask specific individuals in a questioning session and this can be a valuable part of your differentiation or assessment.

Getting some children, especially shy children, to answer a question can be problematic. Give children plenty of experience of interactive lessons, and create a positive atmosphere in which the risks of a wrong answer are bearable. Children are more likely to be involved if they feel confident that a wrong response will not elicit criticism or ridicule from you or other children.

Prompting can be useful to help children answer questions. There are three kinds of prompts:

- *verbal* prompts: these include cues, reminders, instructions, tips, references to previous lessons, or giving part sentences for children to complete;
- *gestural* prompts: the teacher models the behaviour of children in order to pre-empt any mistake, e.g. by pointing to the object they want a child to use, or showing how to hold a pen correctly;
- *physical* prompts: these may be necessary among young learners, e.g., if the child cannot yet hold a crayon or form letters or numbers, you can take their hand and guide them.

Vary your acknowledgement of a child's response according to the confidence with which they gave it: a correct, quick and firm response must be acknowledged in a businesslike way (a nod or a gesture), although lower ability and less self-confident children may need more praise. When a child answers a question correctly but hesitantly, give them more explicit feedback to reassure them that the answer was correct and help them remember the correct response. If several of the children seem hesitant you may be asking questions that they do not understand and may need to backtrack to make sure they are with you.

There are two types of wrong answers – those due to carelessness or lack of effort, and those due to a lack of understanding or knowledge. In both cases you need to show that the answer is wrong in a businesslike way without resorting to personal criticism. If an answer shows carelessness or lack of effort, move on quickly to the next child – the denial of possible praise is the best response to a lazy answer. Where there is lack of understanding or knowledge, prompt the child by simplifying the question (perhaps breaking it into a series of small steps) or hinting. If this fails, look to the next respondent for the correct answer, rather than giving it yourself. If a child gives a partly right answer, first make clear the part that is correct and the part that is not, to avoid confusing the child or the class. Then prompt the child to correct the incorrect part of the answer. If this does not work, ask another child to correct or develop the part-answer.

PRACTICAL TASK PRACTICAL TASK **PRACTICAL TASK** PRACTICAL TASK **PRACTICAL TASK**

Focus on your questioning. A really simple practical task you can do with your teacher is to ask him or her to observe a session where you question a group of children. For each box the observer should tick the type of question you asked and whether you asked a boy or girl.

Question type	Sex of child asked
Open	Boy
Closed	Girl

Discuss the results of this and consider whether you need to monitor the balance of your questioning.

Interactive teaching

Interactive teaching is simply varying your teaching so that it engages the maximum number of children. Interactive teaching enables you to address children's learning through different sensory channels and to elicit responses from as many children as possible. This means you can make assessments of more children

Teachers in schools are currently concerned that children learn through a number of sensory channels: visual, auditory and kinaesthetic. Traditionally, we teach relying heavily on the auditory channel by telling children and expecting them to listen. However, it has been suggested that teachers should use more visual learning (based on looking) and more active, kinaesthetic learning. This may suit both the learning style of some children and the different learning requirements of different tasks.

Whenever you are talking to or questioning a group of children, ensure that as many as possible are engaged with you, are responding and are active. Use:

- **small whiteboards on which answers can be written;**
- **talk partners, where children discuss a proposition in pairs for 20 seconds before responding;**
- **phonic or number fans to indicate responses;**
- **picture sorting cards and artefacts that can be held up in response to questions.**

These strategies not only allow you to see at a glance how a wider range of children respond but they give children response time and activity, as well as visual cues.

Also consider how you can make even the simplest activity more active. For instance:

- **if you are teaching children to sing the alphabet, give each child a letter card and play 'stand up' so that they have to stand up when their letter name is sung;**
- **use large PE hoops for sorting activities rather than small ones;**
- **do active phonics games or action counting rhymes daily;**
- **when you ask children to identify something in a whole-class lesson, get them to come out and show the others on the whiteboard, interactive whiteboard or text;**
- **look for opportunities in the outdoor classroom – placing objects on a large alphabet mat is a much more engaging phonic activity than doing a worksheet;**
- **act out action rhymes rather than simply singing them;**
- **use active mathematics games for the mental/oral starter.**

You can also make learning more visual by asking children to represent thoughts in a variety of different ways – mind maps, grids, arrangements of objects, collections of digital photos and PowerPoint shows.

Frequently asked questions

1 'On my second placement the teachers do not do the literacy hour in the way my first school did. The phonics is done separately and my teacher does not do shared reading.'

There are lots of different ways of addressing the teaching of English. The PFTL is not statutory and not all schools do a literacy hour. You should make sure you understand the way phonics is addressed and take part in teaching it, in or outside the literacy hour. It is vital that you learn to teach this element of literacy. You can do a check to see that all the elements of effective literacy teaching are being done. Ask your teacher how she or he ensures the children study a wide range of texts. The teacher may well want to do some shared reading. If you are still concerned, discuss this with your mentor, who will probably not be surprised.

2 'I have been observing and working with groups and my mentor wants me to teach the whole class. I am nervous. Help!'

It sounds as if you have reached a point where you need to take a deep breath, plan carefully and – have a go. It is vital to teach the whole class, if only for short bursts like the mental/oral or shared writing initially. If you cannot do this you cannot be a teacher. You should teach the whole class quite early in the placement because the longer you leave it, the harder it is to begin and the harder it is to establish your role in the minds of the children. Review your observations, plan your first attempts carefully and check plans with the teacher. Do not expect everything to be perfect first time.

3 'In my Foundation Stage unit, I don't have the chance to teach the whole class at once. Is this a problem?'

No, your unit probably does not use this organisation for sound educational reasons. Discuss these with your teacher or mentor and try to understand why a whole class grouping is not helpful here.

4 'I did my first science lesson yesterday and it was a disaster. I couldn't keep my eyes on all the children and some were rude and noisy. This was a lesson plan from my course. What am I doing wrong? Will I ever recover?'

Move on – but do not forget the experience. This lesson sounds as if it was too ambitious either for you or for the class at this point in your career. Review what went wrong very carefully: too much going on at one time? Content not right for the class? No monitoring? Too many resources? You might want to review this with your mentor or teacher. Plan the next lesson to avoid the same mistakes. You could help yourself by asking the teacher to work with you in a TA role in your next lesson. Everyone has some poor lessons but you will learn from these as well as from the good ones.

5 'My mentor has asked me to teach some foundation subject lessons but my friend who is doing the same course has not been asked to do this. I think I would rather stick with the core subjects at the moment. Can I do this?'

Check your course expectations for this placement. Unless it specifies you will teach only core subjects you cannot do this. Your mentor may have identified teaching foundation subjects as your current training need. Your training needs will probably be different from your friend's because you and your school are different. I suggest you check your course documentation and discuss it with your mentor and see teaching foundation subjects as a step onward in your professional development.

Setting homework

Setting homework is an important task for you as it allows you to address Standard Q24. Homework is not statutory in schools in England and, indeed, its educational value is dubious in terms of the difference it makes to pupils' academic outcomes. However, it is a very important way of engaging parents in their children's education. It is also valuable in giving parents the opportunity to demonstrate solidarity and support for the school by encouraging and supporting the completion of homework. Homework may also help children to develop their independence, self organisation and responsibility.

To see how much homework children should have in your school, you need to look at the school policy. DfES recommendations suggest that even at the end of Key Stage 2 children should not have more than 30 minutes of homework a day. This homework might consist of:

- **taking books (or story sacks) home to read with parents or a sibling, a practice that has demonstrated benefits even where parents do not speak English;**
- **taking home mathematics games to play with family members;**
- **homework sheets containing simple, planned work that does not demand elaborate resources and that can be done with parents or siblings;**
- **asking children to research a particular topic;**
- **asking children to ask family members questions about a particular topic;**
- **regular learning of spellings or multiplication tables for tests.**

All these count as homework and an Early Years trainee is as likely to set homework in the form of books or story sacks, as a Primary trainee who may set spellings and worksheets.

Make sure you know the school routine for setting homework.

- **When do children take it home?**
- **When does it come back?**
- **Is there any marking to be done? If so, what sort of response is required?**
- **Find out how schools establish expectations in their parents. Most schools will have handouts for parents about topics like using story sacks, reading with your child, learning spellings, etc. Many schools will organise parent workshops to introduce these ideas to parents.**

When setting homework make sure you:

- **give children a reasonable time to complete the work (they may not be able to do all it on the same day) but not so long that they forget it;**
- **explain homework clearly and ensure that any sheets are sent home with brief instructions for parents;**
- **ensure that homework does not need much in the way of resources, as parents may not be able to find them at short notice;**
- **establish a routine that children and parents will remember easily;**
- **set work that everyone has equal access to – you cannot expect parents to drop everything and rush off to the library and not everyone has a computer;**
- **praise children for doing homework – however poor the results the child has made an effort and shown commitment;**
- **have consistent, non-judgemental expectations of all children – if you have set the homework appropriately you should expect all children to achieve it, whatever their social situation;**
- **support children who repeatedly fail to do homework by discussing it carefully, ensuring they understand and, if all else fails, giving them time to do it in school.**

Setting, managing and marking homework is a very small part of your training but it is something you can easily achieve and feel satisfied about.

Professional values and the wider life of the school

As part of addressing the Standards for QTS you will need to demonstrate that you can:

Q3   Be aware of the professional duties of teachers and the statutory framework within which they work.

Q4   Communicate effectively with children, colleagues, parents and carers.

Q6   Have a commitment to collaboration and cooperative working.

Q30   Identify opportunities for learners to learn in out of school contexts.

Q32   Work as a team member and identify opportunities for working with colleagues.

To look further at the responsibilities and professional standards for teachers we suggest you consult the General Teaching Council for England website on **www.gtce.org.uk** This sets out and discusses the values and professional responsibilities of teachers. On placement you will certainly encounter a range of opportunities to display these values.

Some features of school life are discussed in the early chapters of this book – punctuality, attendance at staff meetings and careful preparation. These demonstrate your commitment to your role as a teacher and mentors invariably mention these issues when writing reports about trainees' progress. However, you will have other opportunities to participate in the life of the school. Some of these will be low key, such as greeting parents at the beginning and end of the day and planning interesting displays of work. Others will be very high profile, such as being invited to go with the school on a residential trip to a study centre. Between these two extremes are all the events, routines and celebrations that are part of school life – sports day, Eid, Christmas, book week, the summer play, class assemblies and day trips. Although they may seem a demanding extra dimension on top of daily planning and teaching, these are the events that allow us to share our values and enthusiasms with children. These events are every bit as educative as the formal curriculum and will also promote key skills such as cooperation and flexibility.

You will need to seek out some opportunities. For instance, if you want to know about the work of the governors in the school, you will need to do a little research on the Internet and then arrange a meeting with a school governor, through your mentor. If you are well prepared, you can find out all you need to know in this way.

Trainees often worry about whether they have done enough to address the standards relating to working with parents. You need to ensure you take opportunities to:

- **observe your teacher (and others) interacting with parents on a daily basis at the beginning and end of school;**
- **greet parents yourself (when this is appropriate);**
- **observe at a parents' evening or open day;**
- **discuss with a teacher the school's efforts to involve parents;**
- **ask to look at the literature that goes home from school to parents, including advice about reading with children, spelling sheets and school newsletters or bulletins.**

PRACTICAL TASK PRACTICAL TASK **PRACTICAL TASK** PRACTICAL TASK **PRACTICAL TASK**

Identify your opportunities to take a full professional role. Use the checklist below to identify what experiences you have already had (column 1) then use column 2 to identify some experiences to aim for in your next placement.

Opportunity	Experienced	Identified for next placement
In the classroom		
Attendance register		
School meal numbers		
Welcome parents and carers before and after school		
Deal with absence notes		
Manage the collection and marking of homework (books to read, etc.)		
Set homework		
Create a display in your class		
Create an interactive area in the setting		
Other		
Beyond the classroom		
Set out and use the gym or hall		
Teach in the ICT suite		
Teach on the field or playground		
Go on playground duty		
Attend a staff meeting		
Attend planning meetings		
Attend a whole staff Inset session		
Participate in a parents' evening		
Attend a PTA event		
Participate in a school visit		
Attend a governors' meeting or discuss it with a governor		
Play a musical instrument in assembly		
Run or participate in a class assembly		
Participate in an after school club or coaching		
Take part in a school visit		
Attend sports day		
Participate in a transition visit to a Key Stage 2 or 3 school		
Participate in a book, arts or charity day		
Attend the breakfast club		
Other		

PRACTICAL TASK PRACTICAL TASK **PRACTICAL TASK** PRACTICAL TASK **PRACTICAL TASK**

Identify your opportunities to use a wide range of resources. Use the checklist below to identify what resources you have already used (column 1) then use column 2 to identify some resources you aim to use in your next placement.

Resources selected and used	Last placement	Next placement
Write on a flipchart or whiteboard		
Selected story or poetry		
Use an OHP		
Use a data projector		
Use an interactive whiteboard		
Use a TV programme		
Use a radio programme		
Use a tape recorder		
Use reprographic equipment		
Teach in an ICT suite		
Use ICT for preparation and planning		
Set out and use the gym or hall		
Use the outdoor classroom or field		
Other		

School visits

To demonstrate you can plan for children to learn in out-of-school contexts (Standard Q30) you do not actually have to plan a visit to another setting. Ideally you would do so, working through the following checklist with your teacher. This might be a visit to a museum, gallery, supermarket, DIY store or local park. However, if you cannot arrange a visit with your class you should ensure you use your placement to look at the school policy, collect the information below and read the latest Standards for LAs in overseeing educational visits, the DfEE (1998) *Health and Safety of Pupils on Educational Visits* and the DfES (2002) *Museum and Galleries Education Programme: a guide to good practice*. All are available on the site **www.teachernet.gov.uk/wholeschool/healthandsafety/visits/**.

Checklist for out-of-school visits

Do you have information about?

School's policy on trips to include: • Adult/pupil ratio/supervision • Charging for school trips • Using transport for school trips • First aid/inhalers • Insurance in relation to school trips • Emergency procedures • Exploratory visit by trip leader	
Risk assessment procedures	
Information to pupils	
DfES guidance on health and safety of pupils on educational visits	
LA guidance on health and safety of pupils on educational visits	
Letter/consent form proformas	
Proposal form for HT outlining the objectives, cost, intended leaving/returning times and cost estimate	
Schedule of trips planned for the year across the whole school	
School's procedures on parents' information evenings/sessions in relation to school trips	
Other guidance used in school	
Useful contacts used by the school	
Specific details of a trip already undertaken or to be taken in the current school year	

Communication with parents and carers

As a trainee you will communicate with and report to parents to meet Standard Q4, but you will do this under the supervision of your teacher and only in a limited way. This does not stop you from learning about the processes of communication in your setting. These might include any of the following:

• school newsletters;
• school-run reading or mathematics schemes;
• parent-run projects like story sack workshops;
• the daily communication of meeting parents delivering and collecting their children;
• home visits for those children starting in a new setting;
• parents coming into school to do a regular activity like cooking with children;
• parents or grandparents coming in to talk to pupils about a topic;

- routine parents' evenings or day workshops;
- written reports to parents.

Some of these opportunities are more readily available to you in certain placements. For instance, if you are placed in the Early Years Foundation Stage you are almost certain to have the chance to meet parents or carers and talk to them at the beginning and end of the session. If you are in Key Stage 2, you may only see parents at formal parents' evenings. If you are fortunate enough to be in school for parents' evenings or home visits you should ask to sit in. You will not usually have a real role in reporting but you will be able to observe the teacher at work. Writing reports for parents is a task you should undertake at some time during your placement (Standard Q27). Collect evidence of the attainment of a few children and write mock reports, using the school system. Guidance about your statutory duties and examples of report writing are available on the QCA website, **www.qca.org.uk**

Completing school-based tasks

As part of your training you will almost certainly have a range of placement tasks that are an important part of your learning experience. These may be tasks arranged by your mentor to ensure you have appropriate learning experiences. They may be tasks connected to assignment or dissertations or they may be tasks set by your course tutors to contribute to your development and, possibly, your taught sessions. It would be easy to see these tasks as a distraction from the business of teaching but they do help to ensure you have the necessary range of experiences to meet the standards or to complete academic parts of your qualification. Never ignore these tasks nor leave planning them until the placement is well underway. Plan these tasks right at the beginning of the placement so that you can see what you have to do week by week, then build them into your timetable for the week. If you are undertaking school-based tasks or a research project in school there are some key points to think about at the start of the placement.

- **Ensure you are totally clear about what school-based tasks or projects you need to accomplish during the placement. Although other tasks may well be suggested as part of your training, those you start out with are essential. If you don't plan for them you won't accomplish them.**
- **Review the aims and scope of your tasks or project and ensure you can achieve them in the time available. Make sure, if you are addressing a particular research question, that you are clear how you will collect evidence. If you have school-based tasks, be clear about how much written evidence you need.**
- **Look at your course documentation or talk with your mentor to establish what proportion of time you should spend on your tasks or study. You can then negotiate appropriate times around your teaching commitments.**
- **Check that you are able to work with the resources or pupils you need. Sometimes school plans change suddenly and you may need to re-negotiate.**
- **Where there is background reading or research to do to prepare for your tasks or study, ensure you have done as much as possible before the placement. In this way your tasks will be well focused and you will waste less of your precious time.**
- **Check that any research you want to carry out with children or teachers in your school is ethical and professionally appropriate. If you are part of a course based in a university or college, the institution will have guidelines on this.**
- **Review your project or tasks and list the school staff you would like to talk to or observe. If you are ready with this list, you can discuss it with your mentor.**

Some tasks will be routine teaching that you would do anyway, others may encourage you to focus on a particular aspect of the curriculum or a group of children. Consider each task carefully and be clear about what you will need to do to accomplish it.

For example, a task may require an in-depth look at a small group of pupils. Now is the time to ask yourself some questions.

- **Have you identified this group?**
- **Are these pupils from your own class or will you need to identify pupils from another class or age group?**
- **Have you spoken to your mentor about arranging a visit to another class and to the teacher concerned?**
- **Do you know where the individual pupils fit into the academic range of the class?**
- **How much time is needed in order to carry out these tasks?**
- **Have you discussed them with your class teacher and school mentor?**
- **Have you planned time in which you can carry out these tasks?**
- **Once you have carried out the tasks, will you need to set aside time to complete any writing up?**
- **Consider whether you should share this information with anyone and how you will ensure it is confidential.**

Discuss your school-based tasks with your mentor early on in your placement and monitor them at mentor meetings. This is a very good opportunity for you to demonstrate a professional, organised approach to your work. If you are planning and working through school-based tasks you appear very much more organised and competent than if you leave them until the last fortnight then panic.

If you are doing a project or study involving the children or teachers in your school you will have to make decisions about how far you share data you collect with the children or teachers. Whatever you decide, you should ensure that you have the full consent of all participants in any study and that you anonymise the names of pupils, teachers and schools in such a way that they cannot be identified in any report or dissertation.

REFLECTIVE TASK
REFLECTIVE TASK

Audit the range of:

- **pupil groupings;**
- **resources;**
- **interactive learning strategies (questions, etc);**

you have used on placement so far.

Complete the chart on page 75 with your examples.

Learning objective	Pupil grouping	Resources (including e-resources)	Interactive teaching/ learning strategies
	Whole class or group		Small whiteboards
	Individual pupil	Self-selected book	
	Ability group		
	Mixed ability group		

Which opportunities have you missed so far? When can you plan to try out a grouping or teaching strategy you have not used so far?

A SUMMARY OF **KEY POINTS**

> Being well prepared and appearing confident are key factors in successful teaching.

> You should ask a range of question types and ensure you question a whole range of children. Questioning is a skilled business and you can practise and improve your questioning so that it is a useful differentiation tool.

> Interactive teaching means involving children actively in their learning. It can increase learning in whole-class and group settings. Placement is your chance to develop your use of interactive teaching.

> Homework is a term covering a wide range of activities. Get involved with whatever counts as homework and be thoughtful in setting work for children.

> Professional placement offers a wider range of opportunities for you to demonstrate your values and become involved in the school – seize these opportunities.

> Successful completion of school-based tasks depends on planning for their completion early in your placement.

Resources

To look at the professional roles and responsibilities

www.gtce.org.uk (England)

www.gtcw.org.uk (Wales – in Welsh and English)

www.gtcs.org.uk (Scotland)

www.gtcni.org.uk (Northern Ireland)

Qualifications and Curriculum Authority **www.qca.org.uk** for details of the English National Curriculum.

Department of Education, Lifelong Learning and Skills (Wales) **www.old.accac.org.uk/redirect.html**.

Information for school governors (including roles and responsibilities) can be found on **www.governornet.co.uk**. Look at this site before you meet your governors.

www.teachernet.gov.uk/visits has clear and full guidance about the regulations and practices for school visits including access to DfEE (1998) *Health and Safety of Pupils on School Visits: a good practice guid*e **www.teachernet.gov.uk/wholeschool/healthandsafety/visits/**.

5
Learning to assess, monitor and report on children's progress

By the end of this chapter you should:

- **know the main types of assessment;**
- **know what assessment tasks you need to engage in;**
- **know the role of target-setting.**

Assessing and monitoring

This book summarises some key points about assessment. You need to demonstrate that you have professional knowledge and understanding about assessment, as set out in Standards Q11, 12 and 13. You need to know:

Q11   The assessment requirements and arrangements for the subject/curricular areas.
Q12   A range of approaches to assessment, including formative assessment.
Q13   How to use local and national statistics to evaluate the effectiveness of teaching, monitor progress and raise levels of achievement.

In terms on Professional Skills, you need to fulfil Standards Q26, 27 and 28.

Q26(a)   Use a range of assessment, monitoring and recording strategies.
   (b)   assess the learning needs of those you teach to set challenging learning objectives.
Q27   Provide timely, accurate and constructive feedback.
Q28   Support and guide learners to reflect on their learning, identify progress and emerging learning needs.

You should know what the children can do, note what they have done and identify what they and you need to do next. It is also important to be able to share this information with parents, children and at a school and government level to measure individual, school and national progress. This is the role of assessment. The two main types of assessment you will encounter are *formative* and *summative*.

Formative assessment (assessment for learning, or AFL) is assessment that directly contributes to your teaching. Each time you teach a lesson you assess what the children have achieved relative to your objective. You then act on this by planning the next lesson to take account of how well the children achieved your objective. In Early Years Foundation Stage, a great deal of observation is planned to assess how children are developing in the six areas of the curriculum. This is supplemented by work done by children and records of discussions with children.

Summative assessment (assessment of learning, or AOL) is assessment that gives you a snapshot of the child's achievement at a particular time. It is particularly useful assessment for reporting to parents or to government. The most obvious example is the Statutory

Assessment Tests (SATs) carried out towards the end of Key Stage 2. The results of these are reported to children and parents as a basis for gauging individual progress and are also analysed at school, local and national level. In Early Years Foundation Stage the Foundation Stage Profile helps teachers to collect together all their evidence from formative assessments and make a summative judgement about a child's progress in the areas of learning. This is reported to the parents and school at the start of Key Stage 1. In Key Stages 1 and 2 the statutory and non-statutory tests and tasks are examples of summative assessment.

Assessment is theoretically very simple but is extremely difficult to organise and manage in practice. There are only three things you can assess: what the children know, what they do and what they produce. The simplest ways to assess these things are to:

- **ask children what they know and note what they say;**
- **observe what they do and make notes (or take photos);**
- **collect and annotate what they produce.**

These are your sources of evidence. In practice it is rather trickier than this because teachers are trying to make balanced assessments of a huge range of skills, knowledge and understanding for all the children in the class. Managing this will always be a challenge. On placement there are a number of key assessment and recording experiences you should seek to have, although you might not have all of these in early placements.

Giving feedback and making assessments

Giving feedback and making assessments as you teach is vital and addresses Standard Q27. This sort of assessment should be part of your teaching from the outset. You need to be clear when giving feedback. Do not praise wrong answers. Indicate that they are wrong but do not dwell on them. Where an answer to a question is partially correct, emphasise the correct part. Where a child has an obvious misconception you need to explore this and find out why. Praise children often but not effusively so that praise is seen as a reward.

Recording attainment on your lesson plans

This is a basic type of assessment you can start right from the beginning of the placement. The key to this is identifying clear statements of what you are looking for in your lesson plans that will allow you to assess who achieved the objectives of the session (or lesson).

For example, in one particular lesson you may find that a large number of children found the objective too challenging. In response, you have to amend your next lesson to revisit some aspects of the earlier content. Alternatively, you may find that the objective was not challenging enough for some children and realise you have to provide more challenge for them in the next lesson. This is good teaching and a canny trainee will make quite sure that mentors can see that you do change your lesson plans in response to the outcomes of previous lessons. Some trainees deliberately highlight changes to lesson plans to emphasise that their responses to assessment are to do something in their teaching.

Recording the attainment of the whole group

This is the next step. To do this you can use a class or group grid, which will give you a very easy recording format but little detail. You can use a system of ticks or stars to show how well the objective has been addressed. This format should be adapted as appropriate, with columns and headings to suit circumstances. Records should be dated, systematic, regularly updated, manageable and should clearly summarise learning and inform future teaching. Names of pupils may be arranged to reflect class groupings and should be confidential.

Comments on significant individual responses may also be evident in lesson/activity plan assessments and evaluations with points considered for the next lesson/activity.

Class/Group	Subject/Area of Learning...............................
Names of Pupils	Experience and Achievement

Compiling a pupil profile

A pupil profile will give you an overview of an individual child and also show you just how much varied evidence you need to make judgements about performance. You may well be asked to do this for a number of pupils as a directed task on placement.

Pupil profile (Key Stage 1 or 2)

Name of pupil ....   **Class** ....

This record is designed to reflect pupil progress during the placement:

- **to contribute to the school's own pupil records;**
- **to provide evidence to support reporting to parents.**

This record may be adapted to suit the balance of areas taught:

Subject	Comments *(dated entries to record key points in learning)*
English	
Mathematics	
Science	
ICT	
PSHE/Citizenship	

RE	
D&T	
History	
Geography	
Art	
Music	
PE	

Key targets for pupil's development:

- **completed by end of school experience;**
- **based on evidence in profile above.**

Pupil profile (Early Years Foundation Stage)

Name of pupil ....   **Class** ....

This record is designed to reflect pupil progress during the placement:

- **to contribute to the school's own pupil records or Early Years Foundation Profile;**
- **to provide evidence to support reporting to parents.**

This record may be adapted to suit the balance of areas taught.

Area of learning	Comments *(dated entries to record progress in learning)*
Personal and social development	
Language and literacy	
Mathematical development	
Knowledge and understanding of the world	
Physical development	

Creative development	

Key targets for pupil's development:

- **completed at end of school experience;**
- **based on evidence in profile.**

Levelling children's work

Levelling children's work against the criteria (statements of attainment) for national curriculum levels is very important and something that you may seek out a little later in your experience. To do levelling you need to identify your subjects, select a range of examples of work, notes of observations and discussion with the child and ascribe a level against the national curriculum statement of attainment criteria. These are available as part of the national curriculum but in the case of mathematics and English have been considerably elaborated in the handbooks of the statutory tests. Levelling children's work involves the idea of best fit, where a child will have features of a number of levels in its work but will have most in one level – the level that best describes the child's performance. You should do this task, initially, with the support of your teacher or mentor.

Observing the administration of statutory tasks and tests

This will be important whatever age phase you are training to teach. These tests and tasks are used to provide a summative (or snapshot) assessment of children's achievements at the end of the key stage. The tests take place in English (but only reading, writing and spelling), mathematics and science. There is an additional English task at Key Stage 1 that is done with each child over a prolonged period.

To ensure you know the arrangements for each year's tests and tasks, consult the QCA website where you will find the assessment and reporting arrangements for Key Stages 1 and 2.

If you are an Early Years trainee you should observe the Key Stage 1 tasks and tests during the summer term placement. The Key Stage 1 reading task takes place over a long period of time. It contains a running record, which is a very important assessment technique. You should ensure you understand the process of doing a running record by reading the teacher's handbook from the tasks pack. You should also do a trial, or mock, running record with at least one child. If you are a Primary trainee you should observe both the Key Stage 1 and Key Stage 2 tasks and tests and the comments about the running record, above, also apply to you.

Naturally, statutory tasks and tests may not be taking place in your class. You should talk with your mentor and arrange to visit the classes where the tasks and tests are happening.

It is not enough to observe how the tests are administered. You must also understand how they are marked and how those marks are used. Whichever tests and tasks you observe, please take the time to look through a test and task handbook so that you know what you are seeing and how the marks are arrived at. You can ask to look at the teacher's marking for the Key Stage 1 tests but Key Stage 2 tests are externally marked and you cannot have experience of marking them. However, if you are a Key Stage 2 trainee, you should ask to mark a few of the non-statutory optional tests that most schools use in Years 3, 4 and 5. This will give you experience of the close guidance and precise marking that is called for.

Contributing to the EYFS Profile or school reports

This is a very important aspect of assessment. You need to collect a wide range of evidence and ensure that your comments highlight what the child has achieved and what is now the target. You should write some mock Early Years Foundation Stage Profile entries or reports (perhaps using the school report software) and scrutinise these with your teacher or mentor. If you are unsure of the format, QCA gives very clear guidance about what should be included in school reports in the assessment and reporting arrangements for Key Stage 1 and Key Stage 2 and principles and examples of good report writing at **www.qca.org.uk/ 120-6227.html** The full handbook for guidance about the Early Years Foundation Stage Profile for children completing the Early Years Foundation Stage is also available on **www.qca.org.uk/**

QCA gives the following advice about writing reports:

- **The report should be written for parents in a clear and straightforward way. However, schools should be mindful that the majority of pupils will read their report.**
- **The report should be personal to the pupil.**
- **The report should be written in plain English and legible. Comments should be as succinct as possible, using words that are precise and appropriate.**
- **Jargon should be avoided if it is likely to be misunderstood.**
- **Reports should indicate whether or not the child is happy, settled and behaving well.**
- **The report should advise parents how they can help and support their child.**

Points applicable to individual subject reports
- **The report should give an indication of attainment and progress within the subject areas covered during the year – it should be general enough to suggest breadth and specific enough to give parents a clear understanding of the progress made by their child.**
- **The report must include a national curriculum level when there is a statutory requirement to report a level at the end of the key stage. This information may be presented on a separate sheet.**
- **The report does not need to include a national curriculum level other than at the end of the key stage.**
- **The report should indicate how the pupil's work compares with the average for pupils of their age.**
- **The report should indicate effort as well as attainment.**
- **The report should indicate strengths and areas for improvement.**
- **Where there are specific suggestions for how to improve or targets, these must be clear to the pupil.**

Setting targets for children

During school experience you will also be expected to use your records of assessment to set realistic and demanding targets for your pupils.

You also need to be aware of government targets, e.g. in areas such as English and mathematics, as well as school targets based on a variety of data including schools' test scores in relationship to those of similar schools – *benchmarking.*

It is now a legal requirement for schools to set improvement targets in core curriculum areas, and they are encouraged to do so in other aspects of school life. You will find that teachers in schools have been setting targets for several years, so you will become aware of the processes they employ when seeking school and pupil improvement.

Setting targets in the classroom

When setting targets in the classroom, you should consider:

- **school targets (obtain a copy of the relevant information);**

- issues affecting the whole class (academic and non-academic);
- issues affecting groups within the class (academic and non-academic);
- issues affecting individuals within the class (academic and non-academic).

Consult your class teacher or mentor about these.

Setting targets for classroom improvement

When setting targets with pupils, the process already established for your own target-setting may be used, with minor changes. You will need to start with pupils' current knowledge, understanding, skills, behaviour patterns, etc. – review. However, in place of the standards for QTS you will need to consider targets and policies already in place within your school, key stage or classroom – school targets. The rest of the process follows the same route as your own target-setting.

The nature of target-setting with pupils varies. Some targets will be long-term and may feature school priorities that are in the challenging zone. You will almost certainly need to work through the planning cycle (Figure 5.1), record your plan and share it with all those involved. On other occasions, for example after marking pupils' work, it might be sufficient to agree a target in the comfort zone with the pupils and write it on the board or in the pupils' books.

As you get used to the target-setting process, you will be able to use the key headings as a checklist and begin to write down only what is necessary. Whenever possible, try to involve pupils in setting targets so that eventually they will be able to use the process for themselves.

Figure 5.1. Target-setting as part of a cycle for improvement

Working with elements of the cycle

Reviewing

Before you set targets with your pupils you need to review with them their current performance in the area designated for improvement. Evidence relating to how well pupils are doing may be obtained from a variety of sources and used when setting individual, group or whole class targets. You might consider, where appropriate:

(a) pupils' exercise books, pictures or work folders;
(b) records of assessments made by you, your teacher and other practitioners;
(c) displays of pupils' work;
(d) comments made by the class teacher or other colleagues, including annotations on saved work giving the context and task;
(e) your own observations within and outside the classroom;
(f) the pupils' comments related to the proposed area for development;

When reviewing you should:

(a) use appropriate evidence of pupils' current performance;
(b) discuss the current situation with pupils and obtain their perspective. You could get them to carry out a simple self-evaluation.

Working with school targets

Schools will have established their own targets and you will need to find out what these are and feature them in target-setting with your pupils. There will be some targets that reflect national priorities such as English and mathematics. These will have been set when schools analysed the data from their annual tests. The national data, known as the Autumn Package, are produced jointly with OFSTED and QCA and are available on the QCA website. They contain national summary results, value added information and benchmark information. The Pupil Achievement Tracker (PAT), a package of software, allows schools and LAs to analyse their own pupil performance data against national performance data published in the Autumn Package. Further details are available at **www.qca.org.uk** There are four main areas of analysis possible in PAT:

- **school level analyses comparing the school results in the key stage tests and teacher assessments with schools similar to them (in terms of either eligibility for free school meals or prior attainment);**
- **pupil level value added – comparing the progress of individual pupils or groups of pupils between key stages (or within key stages if the school has pupils' optional test results) with progress nationally;**
- **question level analysis allowing schools to see how their pupils performed in each of the questions in the national curriculum tests compared to performance nationally – so that teaching can address those test questions where pupils have performed poorly.**

PAT also helps the school to set targets for individual pupils in the light of projections based on progress by similar pupils in the best performing schools with a similar baseline. You need to discuss this with the responsible person in your school to meet Standard Q13, which specifies that you should know how to use statistical information.

Each teacher will be expected to contribute to the achievement of these targets. This will mean setting targets at the appropriate level for the pupils in the class. Where targets are long-term, it will be necessary to break them down into manageable steps.

You may not know the full details of school targets but you should aim to find out what those targets are and how they affect your class.

When working with school targets you should:

(a) find out what the school's targets are and how they relate to the school's performance data;
(b) discuss with your class teacher what the appropriate targets for the pupils in your class are and how these are being addressed;
(c) ensure that targets you set with pupils support, rather than conflict with, school targets and aims.

Target-setting

You will be asked to identify with the pupils, clear and measurable targets that take them forward from their current performance. When schools set targets they are encouraged to think SMART: **s**pecific, **m**easurable, **a**chievable, **r**ealistic, **t**ime related.

They are also asked to set challenging targets in areas of high priority – targets in the challenging zone, as well as those where success is readily achievable – targets in the comfort zone. You may set targets for the whole class, a group or individuals. The targets may be in academic or non-academic areas and be short- or long-term.

When setting targets you should:

- consider your review of pupils' work and pupil self-evaluation;
- consider school targets, class targets, etc.;
- write lesson/session/day targets (or learning objectives) clearly on the board;
- make long-/medium-term class targets (e.g. rules) clearly visible and refer to them;
- make individuals' targets clearly visible, e.g. use a particular colour when you or they write targets in their books (some non-academic targets can be written on small cards and taped to the pupils' tables);
- communicate with parents on a daily basis, sharing the targets with the home and let parents know of successful achievements;
- make your targets:
  – SMART;
  – in the challenging as well as the comfort zone.
- make certain that the pupils have a clear picture in their minds of what success will look like. Get them to tell you what they understand to be a successful outcome. Check that it matches your criteria.

Developing strategies

You now need to think of ways to put your carefully framed targets into action. When developing strategies to improve pupils' performance, you may consult with mentors, tutors and other students, read appropriate articles and books, or brainstorm. However, when working with pupils you will mainly be discussing their targets with them. If possible let them make suggestions and thus acquire some ownership of the strategies about to be implemented. You must be careful to avoid dashing into action with your first idea without considering its implications or alternatives that might be more promising.

When developing strategies you should:

- consider a number of possible courses of action and include pupils in discussing them;

- select actions most likely to succeed;
- consider what support you will need to implement the plan;
- list any resources you will require to implement the plan;
- when necessary, have a timetable for implementing the various parts of the plan.

Taking action and monitoring progress

While implementing your strategies, you will need to check that you are on track by review-ing and monitoring progress made by the pupils. You may wish to enlist the help of the pupils in keeping records of their progress. In doing this you can be creative in designing, or encouraging pupils to design, appropriate recording sheets. You will find that some pupils will be used to discussing their progress and will be developing their understanding and language about this while others will have less experience and find it hard to monitor and discuss their progress. Even the youngest child in the Early Years Foundation Stage can begin to plan, do and review what has been done and that reflection can be learned early on.

When monitoring progress you should:

(a) consider with the pupils their progress against the targets, using records as evidence;
(b) consider with the pupils progress in relation to the time scales;
(c) decide if you need to reconsider your strategies with the pupils;
(d) decide with the pupils if you need to modify the targets.

Actively involving children

When working with children you should try to increase motivation by giving them some ownership of the target-setting, monitoring and recording processes. Celebrate children's success. How does the school do this – awards, certificates, stickers, displays, etc.? Discuss this with teachers, mentors and children. You can set and celebrate targets in many aspects of school life. Be creative.

Always be aware of the importance of recognising success when pupils achieve their targets. This reinforces desirable behaviour patterns, helps to develop self-esteem and encourages even greater effort. Children's achievements need to be recognised across the curriculum and opportunities for success must be provided. Work needs to be differ-entiated so that it is set at an appropriate level and there is also the element of challenge. This enables children to strive for and achieve success (see Figure 5.2).

REFLECTIVE TASK
REFLECTIVE TASK

Plan a discussion with the assessment co-ordinator in your school. Ask some of the following questions:

- **What are the school improvement targets?**
- **How were these targets identified?**
- **Who has been involved in addressing these targets?**

Then consider how the school targets are reflected in the curricular planning for your class.

Appropriate and challenging work

Striving to reach attainable goals

Successful experience

Developing confidence and self esteem

Further motivation

Figure 5.2. Achieving success

A SUMMARY OF **KEY POINTS**

> Assessment and monitoring of pupil performance begins with clear planning. Ensure your assessment criteria are included in your plans and evaluate them.

> Assessment, planning, target-setting and teaching are processes in a cycle that generates learning and school improvement.

> Schools, classes and pupils will all be working with targets for improvement and you need to know what these are.

> You will need to discuss target-setting in school with your teacher or mentor at two levels – whole-school targets and how your class are addressing these; and targets for individuals and groups in the class.

> There are key assessment experiences you should have at some time in your placements. These include routine evaluations and record keeping, levelling of children's work in various curriculum areas, completion of pupil profiles, completion of school reports, contribution to the Early Years Foundation Stage Profile and observation of statutory tasks and tests.

Resources

DfEE (1997) Setting Targets for Pupil Achievement: Guidance for Governors.

QCA (1999) *Keeping Track: Effective ways of recording pupil achievement to help raise standards*.

See also the Training and Development Agency (TDA) website **www.tda.gov.uk**.

Details of the assessment and reporting arrangements for Key Stages 1 and 2 are available at **www.standards.dfes.gov.uk/**.

Details of the Pupil Achievement Tracker are available at **www.standards.dfes.gov.uk/performance/**.

Many local authorities have produced their own guidelines on target-setting. Try to acquire a copy.

6

Individualised training: target-setting, observation and assessment on placement

Teaching placement is different for every trainee. You have a unique background and experience and each class you encounter is different. In this section we examine key issues for you as a trainee – how your placement is shaped, directed, monitored and assessed. You need to understand these processes to use them purposefully.

By the end of this chapter you will:

- **know what to expect when you are observed;**
- **understand the role of target-setting in your professional development and how to set targets;**
- **know how to prepare for, conduct and follow up mentor meetings;**
- **be able to manage and prepare for your assessment against the standards for the award of QTS;**
- **recognise the link between your placement and your professional development as an NQT.**

Observation

One of the most useful experiences you can expect to have as part of your training is to be observed teaching. It is also one of the most realistic professional experiences you will have because teachers are observed throughout their careers. You will see that teachers in your placement schools observe each other, are observed by subject co-ordinators, head teachers, local authority advisers and OFSTED inspectors.

During your initial teacher training you will be observed by a number of people:

- **your class teacher;**
- **your mentor;**
- **your course tutor;**
- **subject specialists or head teachers in the school;**
- **external and internal examiners;**
- **OFSTED inspectors.**

These observations, and the feedback and target-setting they give rise to, are your chance to address Standard Q9 and show that you can act on advice and be open to coaching and mentoring.

Observation by your class teacher

Most day-to-day observation will be done in an informal way, simply because the teacher is in the classroom with you. Unless you ask otherwise, he or she may give you only a few words of feedback. This sort of observation is valuable as the teacher will build up a comprehensive picture of your performance across the whole range of subjects and in a variety of settings – the class, the hall, the ICT suite, etc. These observations, however informal, will inevitably contribute to your assessment because the mentor is likely to discuss them with the class teacher.

You can focus these observations so that they work for you. Ask your teacher to observe you in specific sessions where you are addressing one of your targets, whether it is to teach in the ICT suite, to manage children positively in the outdoor classroom or to use a more varied range of questions. You will need to discuss your plan and give a copy of it to the teacher as part of the observation. When giving you feedback your teacher will pick out what you did well and suggest things you can do to continue progress. He or she will certainly see that you are focusing on improvement and looking for advice and this, in itself, is good practice. It would be unrealistic to expect full, detailed feedback for every lesson or session you teach and you should not assume that a lack of comment from your teacher indicates something negative. If you would like your teacher's insights about some aspect of your teaching and you have not asked him or her to observe the session, make sure you ask specific questions. Questions like 'What did you think about the worksheet I used?' or 'Do you think the tasks were at the right level for blue group?' are much more likely to have useful answers than general questions like 'How did it go?'

MINI CASE MINI CASE **MINI CASE** MINI CASE MINI CASE **MINI CASE** MINI CASE

Actually teaching in front of my teacher on first placement was agony to start with. I just hadn't expected it, really. The worst bit was that I was desperate for feedback. No – for praise. I only wanted to hear good stuff. If my teacher didn't say 'That was good' I felt despondent and I hung around hopefully at the end of every lesson. After the first week I got used to it and could discuss lessons rationally and even accept tips for the future, which was her way of giving advice. In my second week my teacher gave a sort of wave and nipped out of one lesson. I think it was the first time I realised that she wasn't scrutinising my every movement. It also made me realise I was in charge – at least for a bit.

Harbahavan, PGCE Primary.

MINI CASE MINI CASE **MINI CASE** MINI CASE MINI CASE **MINI CASE** MINI CASE

In my first class I was totally relaxed about teaching in front of my class teacher because I'd worked in her class for a while. She offered reassuring comments whenever I taught. I wasn't really prepared for how different it would be when I went to another class on placement. Initially, I felt nervous teaching in front of someone else but I got used to it quickly. It was harder to get used to the way he often didn't comment about my teaching every time I taught a lesson. I found myself asking 'How was it?' all the time. As the placement went on, I realised that my teacher did comment, but just not about everything I taught and I relaxed about it. I also found that he was really pleased to be asked to observe a lesson and talk through the good and bad points after – he just liked to be asked to do it. I think he really didn't want to be over-critical and make me feel I was being observed in every lesson. The placement went really well and I learned a lot from that teacher.

Maureen, GTP.

Observation by your mentor

Your mentor, or sometimes your class teacher, will do more formal observations. The number of these will vary but you can expect about one formal, written observation a week, including those of the course tutor and other staff, over the length of your placement. You will agree times for these in advance and make sure a copy of your planning for the session or lesson is available to your mentor at the start of the observation. These observations will usually be recorded on a sheet with a specific format (although these vary from course to course) and comments will be linked to the standards and your targets. You will be given a copy of the feedback shortly after the observation and have a chance to discuss the observation with your mentor in your mentor meeting, if not before.

Some of these observations will be general, in the sense that they are observations of you teaching a particular subject, such as PSHE, or in a particular setting, such as the outdoor classroom. The mentor will pick out particular points, usually relevant to your planning and teaching of the lessons, and link these to the standards. As a result of each observation you will be clear about some things you have done well and, probably, have a target for you to work towards.

Other observations will be focused on your particular targets, either those identified before the placement or those identified at a mentor meeting. You may want a number of observations to address a particular target, such as giving appropriate praise, or using your voice effectively, or maintaining the pace of a lesson. These observations will be particularly good for helping you to be aware of progress towards a particular standard.

Observation by your course tutor

If your ITT provider has course tutors who visit on placement, they will usually observe you teaching. This will be the same sort of formal, written observation as your mentor makes and you will be given the notes and verbal feedback after the observation. The tutor will arrange a visit in advance and will probably ask to see a specific part of your teaching – a particular subject, or teaching in the outdoor classroom. The tutor will want to meet your mentor and class teacher and this might influence the timing of the visit. Tutors will usually arrive slightly earlier than the observation and try to put you at your ease by chatting informally for a few minutes. You should prepare as carefully for tutor observations as you would for a mentor observation. Have a copy of the lesson plan available for the tutor and make sure your placement file and training plan file are available if the tutor wants them. If you are in a Key Stage 1 or 2 class you should probably identify a place for the tutor to sit, so that he or she does not get in the way of the lesson. These details present you as a well organised professional even before your lesson is observed.

The course tutor may well do a joint observation with your mentor, class teacher or head teacher. This means they will both observe you at the same time, with the tutor and mentor making observation notes. Both observers will then discuss the observation between themselves before giving you feedback, including the written notes. The point of an observation like this is to ensure that both the mentor and the course tutor have the same expectations about your performance and that both make the same judgements about your teaching. This is a form of moderation and helps to ensure that all trainees are judged fairly.

MINI CASE MINI CASE **MINI CASE** MINI CASE MINI CASE **MINI CASE**

Tutor observations are nerve-wracking because you don't really know the tutor that well. I was always secretly slightly concerned in case I was different from all the other trainees and just didn't know it!

Ben, PGCE.

> **MINI CASE** MINI CASE **MINI CASE** MINI CASE **MINI CASE** MINI CASE **MINI CASE**
>
> *My tutors were really helpful. They always gave feedback on my plans as well as the sessions. Most of the sessions where I have been observed went really well but one; when I did a Chinese New Year activity with a Reception group, it was a bit of a management disaster. I hadn't really considered that all the glittery things and gold paint would be so exciting for the children. They got a bit giddy and I didn't calm them down. I felt stressed and nervous and panicked a bit and the whole activity was disorganised, with overexcited children and me totally failing to use my key vocabulary or address my teaching objectives. I thought the tutor would be really cross and that I'd totally humiliated myself. Actually, she was fine. She did agree with my evaluation of the lesson (and it was painful to see that in writing) but she was very constructive. We identified a list of things to do to reduce my nervousness and to ensure I managed Foundation Key Stage groups better. Most importantly, my tutor pointed out that not every lesson is going to go well and that sometimes, a disaster might just be the session that is observed. It didn't affect my assessment because other lessons observed were good and the tutor could see from the lesson observation sheets in my file that my mentor had observed good sessions.*
>
> Gina, Early Years PGCE (part-time).

Observation by your subject specialist or head teacher

These sessions will be formal written observations like those with your mentor. It is very useful to have a particular subject co-ordinator or phase co-ordinator look at their area of interest, especially if it is one of your target areas. Their expertise in the subject and also of observing other teachers' lessons will mean they can give you good feedback and new ideas. Prepare for these observations as you would for a mentor observation and make sure your plan is available to the observer.

Observation by your external or internal examiners

All training programmes have examiners of some sort. Internal examiners or moderators may be partnership staff or local head teachers who observe a number of trainees for moderation purposes. They will be observing to check that the expectations and judgements made by mentors and course tutors are consistent for all the trainees.

External examiners will be senior staff from other training partnerships. They perform a similar moderation role on most courses. They observe to ensure that the standards for QTS are being met and that the grades awarded to trainees are consistent, not only across the course but for trainees in other programmes. External examiners will also check that the Standards for QTS are met. Although you might not welcome a visit from an examiner you should not worry. They are very experienced and their visits protect the standard of your award by ensuring that grades are fair.

There are a number of reasons why you might have visits from examiners. All GTP candidates are likely to have an external examiner visit towards the end of their final placement as part of their programme. On an ITT course the most likely reason for a visit is that you have been chosen more or less at random as part of a sample of the cohort. However, if you have experienced severe difficulties and may not achieve the Standards for QTS, then you may also have a visit from the external examiner to collect evidence to inform an examination board. This evidence will be an important part of making the decision about whether you have met the Standards for QTS.

Any visit by an external or internal examiner or moderator will be arranged in advance. They will expect to observe you teaching, talk to you, talk to your mentor or class teacher and look through your placement file and training plan. Make sure these are readily available and that you have a copy of your lesson plan ready to give your visitor. The examiner may give you feedback but you should not automatically expect detailed feedback if the main purpose of the visit is moderation.

Observation by OFSTED inspectors

You may be observed by OFSTED inspectors for two reasons. All ITT provision undergoes OFSTED inspection and so it is possible that you will be observed as part of the inspection of your ITT provider. In this case, you will be notified in advance and the partnership will tell you very clearly what to expect and what you should prepare. The inspector may want to observe you teaching, interview you and the mentor and take a detailed look at your files. Alternatively, the inspector might ask to observe another aspect of training, such as one of your mentor meetings. If you are notified of an OFSTED visit, contact your ITT provider, who will be able to tell you exactly what to expect, how long it will take and who will be involved. Your role is to ensure you are well prepared so that you are organised, professional and confident on the day. It would be unusual for inspectors to give detailed or written feedback after a visit to a trainee but they will usually give some, limited, verbal comments.

You might also be observed as part of the school's OFSTED inspection. As schools receive short notice of an inspection, your placement could well fall in an inspection week. In this case the school will usually advise you about what they would like you to do that week. It is a good time to fit in and work together with the staff. Be prepared to support your teacher in any lessons that are observed or to be observed teaching yourself. Your teaching might well be confined to groups during OFSTED week if your teacher prefers that. Be well prepared for whatever you teach and ensure your files are available. The inspector may want to talk to you about your experience in the school. Remember that while you are not going to be the school's first priority during inspection week, OFSTED will be looking at the provision made for trainees by the school. OFSTED inspectors will always talk to you if they observe you teaching, but you should not expect written feedback or much detail. Having an OFSTED inspection during your placement is a useful experience. You see the school at its best (well prepared) and its worst (nervous teachers). Being part of a school's OFSTED inspection teaches you that inspection is a routine part of school life – and experience of an OFSTED inspection is a great thing to talk about at job interviews.

Target-setting for your training

Throughout your training (and afterwards in your NQT year) you will be expected to set clear targets to help you improve your performance towards all aspects of the Standards for QTS (and, later, induction standards). Target-setting alone will not bring about improvement – it needs to lead to action. This section will help you to set realistic and demanding targets and to think through how your targets can be achieved through effective action.

Reviewing

In order to set your targets for a placement you will need to review and analyse your current performance. Before your first school placement, your mentor or tutors will help you to set appropriate targets based on some general expectations of a first placement but taking into account your previous experience. For example, on first placement, a trainee teacher who has been an experienced nursery nurse might be expected to address Standards Q32 and Q33 and work collaboratively with teaching assistants in a nursery placement, whereas this would be far more challenging for a trainee coming straight from university and going into a Key Stage 2 placement.

If you are setting targets for a second, third or fourth placement, you will start by reviewing the outcomes of previous placements. With your mentor or your course tutor, you will discuss your mentor's placement report from the previous placement, your observation notes, and your placement file and your own self-evaluation to identify your progress and needs. This is not to say that the beginning and end of placements are the only times to review your progress but these are times when you are particularly concerned to set targets.

Progress with the Standards

An essential part of your programme is to achieve all the Standards that lead to QTS. Therefore, during and after each school placement, it will be necessary for you to consider your progress against the particular Standards related to that work (refer to the *Professional Standards for Qualified Teacher Status*). Mentors and course tutors will discuss school placements with you.

When considering Standards you should:

(a) know which Standards you aimed to address during this placement;
(b) look at written feedback related to the Standards, e.g. placement reports, mentor meeting notes, observations;
(c) note oral feedback from mentors and tutors.

There will be some Standards you have not had the opportunity to address (perhaps because you were not in an appropriate age phase or situation) and some that you have not succeeded in demonstrating yet. These would be good candidates for your list of targets to be identified.

Target-setting

The more precise you can be in stating what you want to achieve the easier it will be for mentors and tutors to help you and for you to measure your achievement. Get a clear picture in your mind of what success in achieving your targets will look like by being able to complete the sentence 'I will know I have achieved this target when...'

Finally, set a realistic number of targets at the beginning of a placement and expect that some of them will be ticked off and replaced with new targets during the placement. Others will last for the duration of the placement and be more fully reviewed at the end of the placement. For instance: 'to teach clearly structured, three part lessons in maths, science and English (Q25 a, c and d)' may last all through the placement, whereas 'to know about the requirements and school policy for citizenship (Q15)' may be addressed more rapidly.

At the end of this placement, you should again review your progress and begin target-setting for your next placement.

MINI CASE MINI CASE **MINI CASE** MINI CASE MINI CASE MINI CASE **MINI CASE**

Louise had just completed her second school placement during which she had been placed with a Year 5 class. The placement had gone well and during her time in school she had progressed from taking parts of whole class lessons or group work to sustained periods of whole-class teaching in some curriculum areas. Although she had had to develop a range of behaviour management strategies in order to promote purposeful learning environments, her mentor reported that Louise was sensitive to the needs of her class, demonstrated and promoted positive values and set high expectations. She had developed a pleasant relationship with the children.

Louise's mentor suggested that her targets included:

- **continuing to develop behaviour management strategies (Standard Q31);**
- **learning how to develop liaison between home and school (Standards Q4, Q5).**

Louise understood that her pupils' attitudes and behaviour are influenced as much by their everyday lives outside school as by the time spent in school. Encouragement, support and guidance from both home and school are crucial and can have a significant impact on their learning. Louise appreciated the need for establishing a purposeful learning environment and that she needed a greater range of strategies in order to ensure that her pupils were always interested, motivated and remained on task. This would help them to learn effectively, not disrupt others and make significant progress.

In *Qualifying to Teach: Handbook of Guidance*, Louise read of the importance attached to teachers finding ways to communicate with parents and carers, especially those unwilling or unable to offer adequate levels of support. She also read that to achieve Standard Q31 she must demonstrate a range of strategies to promote good behaviour in a wide range of contexts.

In order to achieve the targets suggested, Louise began to make them more specific.

She arranged focused observations of experienced teachers in order to see how they dealt with specific aspects of behaviour management – settling children at the start of lessons, grouping children for practical activities, managing transitions between phases of the lesson, maintaining a brisk pace, using the voice effectively, using praise and encouragement, asking questions, intervening when children stray off task. She decided to talk through the school's behaviour policy with her mentor at the beginning of her next placement.

When dealing with parents, Louise decided to become pro-active and talk informally with parents collecting their children from school. She decided to ask if she could write trial reports on some pupils and compare her efforts with those of her class teacher. She determined to talk to her mentor about how the school dealt with problems that necessitated formal discussions with parents. She looked forward to attending her first parents' evening.

Finally, at the end of your course, following your final placement in school, you must meet target-setting requirements for completion of your Career Entry and Development Profile. This asks you to set targets for your NQT year. These can be:

- **areas of the standards where you have had little experience (such as a particular foundation subject you have not taught) work in the outdoor classroom or developing your expertise in working with parents;**
- **areas of the standards you found challenging throughout your ITT and want to strengthen, such as behaviour management or the way you use your voice;**
- **areas of interest to you, such as your specialist subject or special needs.**

Mentor meetings, professional relationships and advice

Some of the most important times in your training are your mentor meetings. These review progress, refocus your targets and maintain your progress towards achieving the standards. It is very important that you agree a convenient, regular time and place for these at the start of your placement. You will also want to keep a record of your mentor meetings as evidence of your professional development, the actions you have taken to meet targets and progress in setting new targets. Some courses provide a special form for this (see Figure 6.1 below), but you can use plain paper. Agree with your mentor who will take the notes and check you agree about what is recorded before you conclude the meeting.

Log of BA/PGCE/GTP Trainee–Mentor Meeting		
This record should be maintained by the trainee and signed by both participants. The top copy should go in the placement file, the pink copy in the mentor's training file and the blue copy should be retained for the course tutor.		
Date: 20 June 2005	Trainee: Belinda Noyes, PGCE Mentor: June Smith	St Joseph's Primary School
Focus for discussion: The science observation done this week IEPs School-based tasks		
Summary of discussion: The science observation identified differentiation for the most and least able as something to work on but showed progress in organising resources and managing the children. We talked about the upcoming Book Week and what costume I might try. We discussed the children in my class who have IEPs and how I can incorporate some of the main points from the IEPs in my lesson plans. One of my school tasks is to examine some IEPs.		
Action points (referenced to the standards): Meet Mrs James (SENCO) to look at IEP writer and review some of my lesson plans. June to organise ((Q19, Q20, Q25a). June will observe my literacy next week, looking at the differentiation (Q22, Q25a, Q25c). I will be taking the fairy tales activity on Wednesday and the horror activity on Friday in Book Week. These activities which demonstrate my teaching work (Q6, Q32).		
Signed (Mentor) .... Signed (Trainee)		

Figure 6.1. Sample mentor meeting notes

When you begin a placement you will have a set of expectations for that placement. It is important to ensure that you keep these, and your personal targets, in mind. One way to do this is to work out a rough timetable of mentor agenda items. You will not use them all but it means that you will not get to the end of the placement and suddenly find that you have three days left to do all your school-based tasks, look at the school citizenship policy and teach RE.

On her second placement of five weeks Belinda's planned agendas looked like this (see Figure 6.2):

Week	Routine items	Things I want to focus on if other issues do not arise
1	The requirements for the placement. My personal placement targets. School welcome pack. What I will observe this week, and my first teaching experiences.	The behaviour policy. School SEN policy.
2	My observations so far of core subjects. Plan to get school tasks (pupil profiles) done.	My teaching of group guided reading and the mathematics mental/oral.
3	No meeting	
4	Observations of my teaching in the last fortnight. Progress on school tasks (observing SATs)	IEPs and meeting with the SENCO.
5	Observations of me teaching this week. Concluding school tasks (discuss marking SATs)	My placement report.

Figure 6.2. Agenda items

Assessment of your placement

Your placement will be assessed against the *Professional Standards for Qualified Teacher Status*. Each placement may have different requirements and not every placement will address all the Standards, so it is important you are aware of which Standards will be assessed during your placement. Completing specific school tasks will also be a requirement of the placement.

For a shorter placement, your mentor will usually write a report towards the end of the placement. The format of this varies from course to course, but you will usually be assessed against each section of the Standards for QTS and comments will be made about your progress in each area:

1. Professional attributes.
2. Professional knowledge and understanding.

3. Professional skills:
   – planning;
   – teaching;
   – assessing, monitoring and feedback;
   – reviewing teaching;
   – learning environment;
   – team work.

You may be graded against each section of the standards or against each standard. The grades will usually be:

1 Excellent.
2 Good.
3 Satisfactory with some weaknesses.
4 Unsatisfactory.

Each course will have a slightly different format and grading system, so be sure to review the assessment forms and criteria before the placement. Examples are provided below, but they may be slightly different from those on your training course.

If you are doing a longer placement, you may well have an interim report in the middle of the placement. This supplements the meetings you have with your mentor and ensures you review your placement in good time. If there are any areas for serious concern, you will be aware of them and can work with your mentor to address them.

These interim and final placement reports (profiles, or assessments) will form a valuable part of your training plan as they are evidence that you have addressed certain standards.

The assessment of your placement will be evidence-based. The sources of evidence will be the formal observations of your teaching made during the placement, discussion with your class teacher about what he or she has observed, records of mentor meetings and evidence you have collected in your placement file, including lesson plans, assessment records, mock reports and school tasks. If you are unsure how to demonstrate that you have achieved a standard, the *Qualifying to Teach: Handbook of Guidance* gives more guidance about evidence for each standard.

Extracts from school placement reports

Professional placement 1

Jenny Xi, Year 5

Attendance (satisfactory) unsatisfactory

General comment

Jenny made a difficult start. She found it hard to manage the class and to establish an appropriate working relationship but she was very tenacious and never gave up. She has taken the advice offered by her tutor, mentor and class teacher and made real progress with classroom management. By the last week she had achieved a calm, working ethos and the children listened well.

Professional attributes

	1	2	3	4
Those awarded QTS must understand and uphold the professional code of the GTC by demonstrating the following				
Q1				
Q2			X	
Q3			X	
Q4		X		
Q5				
Q6			X	
Q7		X		
Q8			X	
Q9		X		

Main areas of strength in professional values and practice

Jenny worked hard to improve her teaching by taking advice and acting on it (Q9). Although she was reticent in her manner and very quiet with other teachers, Jenny did gain confidence as the placement developed. She was consistently thoughtful about pupils and had begun to recognise their needs but she still needs a good deal of support in this area

Targets for professional values and practice

Jenny needs the opportunity to make contact with parents and carers and find out about the mechanisms for reporting to them. This should be a priority for the next placement.

Professional placement 2

James Preston, Reception/Nursery Unit
3 Professional skills
Planning (Q2, Q22, Q23, Q24)

James prepared sessions very carefully and ensured that they were differentiated to meet the needs of most of the children. By the end of the placement he was quite familiar with the expected levels for pupils of this age phase and the moderation meetings he attended in preparation for the EYFSP contributed to this. He planned with the team and led the planning meeting in the final week of the placement (Q6). All practitioners worked from his plans successfully. James made his objectives explicit to the children when appropriate and checked well that they understood. He developed his planning for child-led and outdoor activities significantly as the placement progressed and was aware of the health and safety implications of his plans.

On future placements James should ensure his resources are prepared well in advance of sessions. He also needs to explore opportunities for out-of-school learning.

Summary 1 2 3 4

Teaching (Q25)

James has taught in each area of learning and used the EYFS curriculum effectively. He has been very positive in his use of the digital camera and IWB and has included all the children in the setting. James has gradually learnt about the children's existing attainment and has differentiated well to include all. His home group sessions have been well planned and his free flow activities have been stimulating.

Summary 1 (2) 3 4

Assessing, monitoring and feedback (Q26–28)

James used the appropriate assessment strategies. He has learnt to observe and record but still needs to learn to manage his records. He is positive but but focused in his feedback to individuals. He needs to support his more able pupils.

Summary 1 2 (3) 4

Reviewing teaching (Q29)

James can be too self-critical in his evaluation but he has certainly amended plans well in the light of his review.

Summary 1 (2) 3 4

Learning environment (Q30, Q31)

James adopted the team approach to behaviour very effectively. He is caring, considerate and firm. He showed good health and safety awareness.

Summary 1 (2) 3 4

Team work (Q32, Q33)

This has been a huge learning point. James has learnt to plan for colleagues and follow up his plans.

Summary 1 (2) 3 4

Using your professional placement report

When you have your professional placement report you can use it to set specific targets for your next placement, as evidence towards the completion of the Standards for QTS and to inform your completion of the Career Entry and Development Profile.

Problems during placement

In one sense, all placements present problems for you to solve. Education is, in itself, problematic and you, like the children, learn by setting yourself new tasks and problems. Unfortunately, sometimes difficulties can arise during placement that threaten to affect your progress. The very best way to deal with problems is to prevent them arising. This is a matter of being very clear about your targets, your expectations, your course and what your placement school has to offer. You should also know who to go to in the case of difficulties and exactly what to do if you have to be absent from school for some reason. Read your course documentation carefully before you start your placement.

Unfortunately, at some time during your placement you may feel that you have a problem or difficulty with it. If this happens to you there are a number of things you can do.

- The most common areas for difficulties with placements are allocation of placement, relationships with class teachers, tutors or mentors, assessment of your placement and behaviour management in class. There are sections in this book you may find helpful with these issues. Read the relevant section and consider your problem against this background. A little more research may help you solve your problem.
- See any problem as a test of your ability to demonstrate your professional values and practice. This does not make any problem go away, but it does get you in the right frame of mind to solve it positively, and maintain good relationships.
- Think carefully about whether you really do have a problem with your placement. If the issue annoying you is a result of, perhaps, a comparison with a friend, you might be placing undue emphasis on a minor issue. Always consider this possibility. Teaching placement is a very pressurised experience and some people respond excessively to minor irritations.
- You may have problems during placement that are not directly caused by the placement but affect it seriously – illness, bereavement, etc. Make sure you discuss these with your mentor and make the necessary arrangements. Life happens!
- If you feel there is a problem with your placement that is affecting your training, you should talk to your mentor about it in the first instance. Do not let a problem grumble on throughout your placement without saying anything. If you do this you will have a miserable, resentful placement – probably unnecessarily.
- Your mentor really is your first port of call to discuss problems during placement. If you go straight to other members of staff or to the head teacher before consulting your mentor you could cause offence.
- When you raise a problem with your mentor, make sure you do it as a fellow professional. Make sure you do not accuse individuals, become overwrought or apportion blame. State clearly what your problem is and, if possible, suggest possible solutions or ask your mentor to help you identify possible actions. This shows you are really trying to seek a solution.
- Choose your time to raise a problem carefully. Avoid the temptation to share an important issue in passing during break or in the corridor. Instead you might arrange a brief meeting after school or wait for a mentor meeting.
- Your problem may be such that you cannot discuss it with your mentor. In this case you need to decide who to talk to. This depends of the structure of your training. If you have a course tutor this might be the person. If you are in a school-based ITT provider you should check who manages the provision. It is very important that you read your course documentation and talk to the right person – this may be a course tutor, personal tutor, SCITT manager or headteacher.
- If you choose to confide your problem to your class teacher make sure you are thoughtful and professional in the way you do so.
- Whoever you discuss your problem with will treat it confidentially and professionally. You must do the same within school.
- If you feel your problem is serious and you have not been able to resolve it with your mentor and course tutor you should write to your course leader and ask him or her to help you solve the problem.
- Finally, and this really is if all else has failed, your course will have a complaints procedure. You can use this if you feel you have been unfairly treated.
- Accept that schools are not perfect and be prepared to make an effort to resolve problems. Never give up because you have encountered difficulty. Look for ways to get around it.
- Never, never, never just walk out of a placement, whatever you feel. This is always unjustifiable, unprofessional behaviour.
- Congratulate yourself when you are able to resolve problems effectively. This is a real professional skill.

REFLECTIVE TASK
REFLECTIVE TASK

Identify one target for improvement in your professional skills: planning, teaching, assessing, reviewing, learning environment or team work. This target may be one of your key priorities for a first placement or a target arising from a previous placement. An example might be 'To participate in maintaining a clear framework for classroom discipline in my Y2 placement' (Q30).

Review the following issues in relation to *your* target.

- **What is already in place in your setting? (Behaviour policy, observe the teacher to see what *he* does.)**
- **What you know about frameworks for classroom discipline. (www.behaviour4learning.ac.uk)**
- **What opportunities you have identified to work on in this target. (First whole class session, group support work.)**
- **What feedback you can get about your target. (Will your teacher or mentor observe?)**

A SUMMARY OF **KEY POINTS**

> Each trainee's training is different because each trainee is different. Placements are chosen to meet your training needs.

> As you go through your ITT you will compile a training plan (or record of professional development). This will include your achievements and targets. Your targets will help you to address the standards for QTS.

> To make the most of your professional placement you must be sure you know what the requirements of the placement are and what your targets are. You can then plan to achieve them.

> Your mentor is an important person in your training. He or she will help you to set and monitor targets and arrange placement experiences. Your mentor will be involved in your assessment. Mentor meetings are a key training experience and to use them well you should be prepared and keep records of meetings and agreed targets.

> You will be observed teaching on placement by a number of people. Make sure you know why you are being observed and prepare well for your observation.

> Your mentor, class teacher and course tutor may be involved in your assessment. Make sure they have evidence of your achievements and can easily look at your training plan and placement file.

> Your placement assessment is an important document and you will use it as evidence towards the standards and to set targets for future teaching and professional development.

> Professional problems can be sorted out in a professional way. Deal with any problems swiftly and positively so that you can move on and get the most from your placement.

Resources

The Training and Development Agency website is a goldmine of information for you about all aspects of ITT. If you are a trainee you should be familiar with the website **www.tda. gov.uk/** where you will find the Professional Standards for the Award of QTS, the Induction Standards and the Career Entry and Development Profile. There are very useful areas for trainees.

Teacher support line

Provided by the Teachers' Benevolent Fund and supported by the TDA, this is a confidential national 24-hour telephone counselling, support and advice service for teachers. Free to all teacher trainees and teachers in primary and secondary schools in England and Wales. You can now access counselling using e-mail through the website. Simply follow the links from the homepage. Telephone 08000 562 561 or visit **www.teachersupport.info**.

7
The challenges of placement

As your training proceeds you will find some aspects more challenging than others. In this chapter we address some of the significant areas of professional activity on placement. By the end of this chapter you should:

- **know how to prepare for working well with other adults;**
- **know some strategies for managing children's behaviour;**
- **know what to do if you encounter a child protection issue.**

Working with other adults

Some of the Standards for the Award of QTS deal with working with other adults. You will need to demonstrate that you:

1. Professional attitudes
   Q4 Communicate effectively with colleagues, parents, etc.
   Q6 Have a commitment to collaboration and co-operative working.

2. Professional knowledge
   Q20 Know and understand the roles of colleagues.

3. Professional skills
   Q32 Work as a team member and identify opportunities for working with colleagues, showing the development of effective practice with them.
   Q33 Ensure that colleagues are appropriately involved in supporting learning and understand the roles they are expected to fulfil.

On placement you will be working with a range of other adults. They may include adults who do not teach but are extremely valuable members of staff:

- **school secretaries or administrators;**
- **lunchtime supervisors;**
- **school caretakers;**
- **before or after school carers or club managers;**
- **non-teacher coaching or teaching staff.**

You need to find out about the roles of these members of staff and how they affect you. It is important that you establish a similar relationship with them as you have with your teacher, so you need to know details. For instance, how does the school administrator manage the lunch money? How are registers sent to the secretary? How should you manage the transition to lunchtime/after school activities? How do you manage the transition to netball coaching time? What do you have to do to ensure these practices are maintained?

Another category of adults will work with you in the classroom or setting. These will include:

- **early years practitioners;**
- **teaching assistants;**

- school teaching staff such as the SENCO, teachers from other parts of the school such as a behaviour, communication or learning unit, a special needs teaching assistant;
- visiting professionals such as psychologists, support teachers, social workers, etc.;
- parents.

Early Years practitioners

If you are undertaking a placement in an Early Years setting such as an EYFS unit, a Nursery class or Reception class, nursery nurses, practitioners, assistants or facilitators will be part of your placement. They will be part of the teaching team and you will usually do your planning together as a team. At first it may be difficult to identify the differences between the roles of the teacher and other practitioners. All will set up resources, plan activities, make assessment notes and take time out to observe children. All will manage behaviour, deal with incidents and talk to parents. However, the teacher will lead the planning and assessment and manage the overall situation. This is the role you are aiming for, so you too must learn to work well in a team. Practitioners may work as a full time member of the teaching team or in one of the ways described below.

Teaching assistants

Teaching assistants have a vital role to play throughout the Primary phase and there are now more of them in the profession than ever before. Teaching assistants are deployed strategically to meet the needs of the school or particular pupils.

- Some teaching assistants will work with a particular child, as a result of a statement of special needs or a school decision on action for this child. A teaching assistant may have a specific role for a child, or children with EAL. The teaching assistant may work with the child during whole class work, to support their involvement and understanding, and then work with them in a group. The teaching assistant may also work with other children in the group. You will be expected to plan for the teaching assistant's involvement.
- Teaching assistants from a special unit may work with a child who is spending part of the time in the unit and part of the time in your class. In this case you will need to plan with the teaching assistant to ensure continuity and understanding.
- Some teaching assistants will spend all or part of their time working with a specific class, set or classes. This is a regular arrangement that allows you to plan for teaching assistant involvement and to obtain assessment evidence from the teaching assistants.
- Some higher level teaching assistants will supervise the class at agreed times when work has been set for the children and actual teaching is not demanded. They will not usually mark written work. You will need to learn to plan and set work, mark the results and handle the processes of handing over the class and obtaining feedback about what they have done.
- Some teaching assistants will manage and run particular programmes such as the early literacy strategy, additional or further literacy strategies, booster classes for maths, reading recovery, catch-up or another intervention and support programme. These may be school-based programmes and involve the teaching assistant in working both in your class, perhaps during the whole class part of the lesson, and with a specific group in or out of the class for group work. Alternatively the teaching assistant may take children out of class to a more suitable area. It is worth asking the teaching assistant to explain the programme to you and observing at least one of the sessions.
- Teaching assistants may make and prepare resources for you and will put up displays but you must know how much time they have to do this and what demands are reasonable. You must ensure that you ask for resources in good time and do not expect instant miracles or make impossible demands.

As part of your induction you need to find out which teaching assistants work in your class and what their role is. You should do this by asking the teacher first of all, and it would also be useful to ask the teaching assistants to explain their role to you. You should ask:

- **What teaching assistants or Early Years practitioners work in this class or setting?**
- **What is the role of each practitioner or teaching assistant?**
- **If the teaching assistant's role is with a particular child or children, how does this affect others they work with?**
- **Does the teaching assistant have special responsibility for SEN or EAL?**
- **When does each practitioner or teaching assistant work with this class or pupil?**
- **What role does the teaching assistant or practitioner take in planning and assessment?**
- **What role does the teaching assistant or practitioner take in different parts of the sessions? Do practitioners or teaching assistants lead whole class rhyme time, support individuals during the mental/oral and plenaries, work with groups or take groups of children out of the classroom?**
- **What will the teaching assistant/practitioner prepare? Some teaching assistants prepare all the activities for their intervention programme but most will expect to participate in putting out resources for some activities.**

As you build up responsibility for planning sessions and sequences of lessons you will be working closely with other adults. In an Early Years setting this may mean agreeing to the outline planning for each activity and session but some of the detail will be planned by other practitioners. You will need to see this planning so that you know what is happening in the setting, as your teacher would do. In a Key Stage 1 or 2 class you will be planning for teaching assistants. When you are planning for someone else it is vital that you are very clear about what role you want them to play and what you want the children to learn – this is a basic professional role but it is not as simple as it sounds in a busy class. You cannot expect teaching assistants to read your mind and a very common mistake is to make assumptions about what a teaching assistant knows and fail to explain properly what is required. This puts the teaching assistant or practitioner in a difficult position and they may not be able to do what you want.

We recommend you use a planning format such as the one given in Chapter 3 to make sure that the learning objectives (or outcomes) of a lesson are clear, that the teaching assistant knows exactly what language to use, what support to offer and that he or she can record brief assessment information for you. Your teaching assistant may not be used to having a written plan for lessons but you want to make quite sure you are explicit and a planning sheet is one way to do this. Using a sheet like this is useful for all these reasons but it also has a training role for you. If you become used to planning in detail for a teaching assistant early in your career, you are more likely to continue to think through these issues, even when you do not use a planning sheet for teaching assistants.

You will find that many Early Years practitioners and teaching assistants you work with are well qualified and very experienced. This can feel intimidating when you are starting your placement. However, experienced teaching assistants or practitioners are a real asset. You will benefit from working alongside them and learning from their expertise. You are training for a slightly different role, as teacher, and you are not competing with teaching assistants or practitioners. When working with teaching assistants or practitioners you have a responsibility to be professional, well organised and to behave confidently because to do otherwise undermines their work as well as your own.

MINI CASE MINI CASE MINI CASE **MINI CASE** MINI CASE MINI CASE **MINI CASE**

On my first placement in the Nursery unit everyone worked together. Each practitioner planned for one area of learning each week and managed a teacher-directed and a couple of child-led activities each session. We sort of discussed them at the Thursday meeting then planned our own. At first I thought everyone did exactly the same but after a couple of meetings I realised that Jill (the teacher) steered the planning and used the documents and records to plan. She was really leading the planning and also looking at everyone's plans on a Friday. I worked up to it and did it with her.

Sara, PGCE.

MINI CASE MINI CASE MINI CASE **MINI CASE** MINI CASE MINI CASE **MINI CASE**

I was a teaching assistant myself before this course so it has been strange doing the PGCE. In my second placement I had a full-time teaching assistant (Bev) in the Year 1 class. Actually I found planning for her a bit of a burden. I mean it was great having her. I did things I couldn't have done on my own and I know it improved the children's learning but there were days when I felt that planning for her was just the last straw. My own experience as a teaching assistant helped me to be clear about exactly what I wanted Bev to do and to make sure I talked with her before and after lessons. Even that, though, was something I had to practise. I found Bev very reassuring. She was positive and calm but when I was a teaching assistant myself, I never realised that working with a teaching assistant would be an effort.

Molly, PGCE.

MINI CASE MINI CASE MINI CASE **MINI CASE** MINI CASE MINI CASE **MINI CASE**

In my school there are 12 teaching assistants. Some are assigned to particular classes and some to particular children. Two of them are specially trained to do the intervention programmes for struggling children and work with groups outside the class. One of the teaching assistants is something of an expert on guided reading and does a lot of that in Key Stage 1, working in all the Year 1 classes. I worked with two of the teaching assistants, one (Ellie) in class supporting a child with autistic spectrum disorder and one (Nerika) who did guided reading. I planned for Ellie in all my lesson plans as a differentiation issue and so I asked her to look at my daily plans. She supported her child but also the whole group and it was important that they didn't depend on her too much and addressed the objectives themselves. With Nerika, I had to monitor the guided reading and get feedback from her. I found it quite difficult to suggest texts as she knew them better than me. I became confident working with Ellie and Nerika when I convinced myself that I had nothing to prove. Both teaching assistants were very supportive to me.

Jo, PGCE.

School teaching staff

Staff working alongside you in your class may include EAL teachers, the SEN co-ordinator and teachers from specialist units (such as behaviour support). You need to discuss their roles in much the same way as you would the teaching assistant's role. Make sure you know what they aim to do, which children they are targeting and how they work with you. This may mean that they observe and assess certain children, that they support children in doing activities you are teaching or that they plan, in cooperation with you, for slightly different activities for the target children. Specialist teachers may also come into your class to advise you and help you differentiate for certain children.

Visiting professionals

Educational psychologists, curriculum support advisers and social workers may come to your class for a variety of reasons. Their visits may be part of a school policy implementation or there may be concern about particular children. You should discuss the role of each professional with your teacher and, where possible, shadow him/her at meetings in which they are involved. However, some meetings (for instance those about child protection issues) may be confidential and so sensitive that it would not be appropriate for you to attend. In this case you can still discuss the processes for this sort of meeting without discussing the content. Ensure you know the role of each visiting professional you encounter, how their involvement was triggered, how long they have been involved with the class or child and what the likely actions resulting from such involvement will be.

Parents

Parents may also work in your classroom voluntarily. They will not have had the sort of training or experience a teaching assistant has had, so it is doubly important to ensure you know their accustomed role and that you are very clear about what you would like them to do. In some cases parents come in to work on a particular school initiative, such as a story sack project in the Early Years Foundation Stage or a talking book project with juniors. Find out about these initiatives. In other cases parents come in to assist with a certain lesson. For instance, a parent might come in on one morning a week to play the guitar for the class music session or to supervise handwriting with groups of children. Having parents in classes carries certain child protection and confidentiality issues and all parents coming into class will complete a criminal record disclosure process and have a discussion with a member of school staff about maintaining confidentiality.

Management of children's behaviour

Managing the behaviour of the children in your class is a key issue. You need to demonstrate certain standards related to this:

1. Professional attributes
   Q1 Have high expectations and a commitment to ensuring they achieve their potential.
   Q2 Demonstrate positive values, attitudes and behaviour you expect from children.

2. Professional knowledge
   Q10 Have knowledge and understanding of a range of behaviour management strategies and know how to use and adapt them.

3. Professional skills
   Q30 Establish a purposeful and safe learning environment conducive to learning.
   Q31 Establish a clear framework of classroom discipline to manage learners' behaviour constructively and promote self control and independence.

These issues are the bedrock of good teaching because you simply cannot teach successfully if the class is unruly, will not pay attention to you and is not interested in what you are doing.

The school behaviour policy

The first document of interest to you in a new placement is the school behaviour policy. This sets out the school's aims in terms of the ethos and behaviour of the school and the sort of relationships the staff want to establish. It also sets out the strategies that are used, consistently and by all teachers, to establish and maintain a positive ethos and good relationships. Read this document as soon as possible and observe how your teacher implements the rewards and sanctions described in the policy.

Establishing expectations – the class teacher contract

You will undertake your placement in a class or setting run by a successful teacher. The class will be well behaved and working successfully but each class will be slightly different. For a start, each teacher establishes different expectations of the children at the start of the year and enforces these. This is how the children recognise what is acceptable and learn exactly what is not acceptable. Some teachers will explicitly negotiate rules for acceptable behaviour at the beginning of the year, display these on the wall and review them periodically. This is useful because it gives the teacher a chance to discuss rules positively and make clear the point of each rule, such as 'Talk quietly so that others can be heard' rather than 'No shouting'. However, all teachers have an unspoken contract with their class that ensures that the children behave well as long as they are engaged and interested. If either the teacher or children fail to deliver their part of the contract, the balance of good behaviour may break down.

PRACTICAL TASK PRACTICAL TASK **PRACTICAL TASK** PRACTICAL TASK **PRACTICAL TASK**

Observe your class to ensure you know the terms of the unwritten contract between teacher and children – the expectations, rules and sanctions used on a daily basis. Use the questions below as guidance.

- **What are the rules for talking in a session/lesson?**
- **How do children know when to pay attention to the teacher talking?**
- **How does the teacher know when children are bored or not understanding work?**
- **What are the rules about taking turns in talking during a group or class meeting?**
- **What are the rules for moving around the class?**
- **What are the rules for going out of the class during a session/lesson?**
- **What are the rules for moving equipment around?**

Watch the teacher teaching and try to work out the scale of sanctions and rewards in the class. How does the teacher reward good attention or performance? Identify the rewards your teacher uses that you will need to add to the list. Rewards might be:

- **making eye contact with the child;**
- **making eye contact and smiling;**
- **making eye contact and nodding or other gestures;**
- **using verbal rewards (praise) – 'Well done', 'Good', 'Spot on', 'Lovely', etc.;**
- **using small physical gestures such as patting an arm when praising;**
- **giving a token reward – a house point or sticker (these may add up to a larger reward in a school system);**

- drawing the rest of the class or group's attention to good behaviour or work – 'Look at Ben's great picture!';
- putting a reward sticker or points on to a class chart;
- earning 'golden time' or some other privilege;
- sending the child to some higher authority to show good work (such as the deputy head);
- mentioning or rewarding good behaviour in a key stage or class assembly.

Each time the teacher uses one of these rewards, as he or she does hundreds of times a day, it ensures that the behaviour that was praised or rewarded is more likely to occur again.

- **What does the teacher do when a child does not meet the expectations of the teacher in terms of behaviour? Here are some sanctions:**
- making eye contact with the child;
- making eye contact and frowning;
- making eye contact and nodding or other gestures;
- using the name of a child who is misbehaving to get their attention;
- using verbal sanctions – 'Please don't…', 'Not now', etc.;
- not giving a token reward – a house point or sticker;
- giving a token punishment such as writing the child's name on the board (there will usually be a system of how many names are acceptable in a day);
- spending a minute or so away from activities (time out);
- drawing the rest of the class or group's attention to poor behaviour or work – 'What should Ben do?';
- taking a child aside for a quiet word about unacceptable behaviour;
- keeping a child in class during playtime;
- sending the child to some higher authority to prevent disruption (such as the deputy head – but never send a child out of the class unaccompanied);
- calling another teacher to come and fetch a child.

When you observe your teacher, take about 20 minutes to keep a tally of how many rewards are given out (tiny little things like a word or a gesture) and how many sanctions are used. You will invariably find that many more rewards are used than sanctions. This is called 'catching them being good'. If you find yourself beginning to nag at children, continually criticise or keep repeating the same names you need to check whether you are being very negative. This will not change behaviour. Start to scan the class routinely every minute or so and catch someone being good. The reward of a smile, a nod or a well chosen word does more to establish good behaviour than nagging.

The list of rules, rewards and sanctions you compile is essential knowledge in any class if you are to step into the teacher's shoes.

Acting like a teacher – your part of the contract

As a trainee you want the children to see you as the teacher and respect you as a teacher. Children are certainly not afraid of their teachers so why do they respect and behave well for them? Firstly, because teachers act like teachers, sending out all sorts of subtle signals that indicate they know what they are doing, have authority and expect children to behave well. You need to send out these signals if you want the children to recognise your authority. Here are some strategies for acting like the teacher in a class or Early Years setting.

- **Know the children by name. If you know names you have a good start. 'Please sit down, Jamie' is so much more authoritative than 'Please sit down, no, not you, *you*'. If necessary label children with stickers with their names on. Thank and praise children by name, too.**
- **Look like a teacher – this does not mean a new wardrobe, just sensible choices that show you recognise the dress code in the school and fit into the teacher category of adults.**
- **Move confidently and avoid skulking in the background. If you are feeling nervous, stand up so the children can see you, rather than sitting down.**
- **Use your voice confidently. Your voice is your best tool and needs to vary in pace, tone, pitch and volume. The children respond to changes in your voice, not shouting. So sometimes dropping your voice to a whisper attracts attention better than shouting.**
- **Make sure you have a signal for getting the attention of the whole class. If your teacher uses clapping, hands in the air or a tambourine, you should start by using that signal even if it is not really your style. Everyone develops their own attention-grabbing signal eventually. Some teachers say 'OK, right!', 'Children!', 'Listen, please'; some snap their fingers, clap and sing to get attention. You may not find out what your personal signal is until you hear the children imitating you. All are effective when used confidently.**
- **Do not begin to talk to the class or group until they are silent. Wait, even if it seems to take ages. If you talk while the children are talking it signals that it is acceptable to ignore you and that you are not a real teacher.**
- **Know the systems in the class or setting. If you do not know something make sure you ask the children to tell you in a confident manner. 'Jennie, please put this buggy away where it belongs' is confident. 'I'm not sure where these go – do you know?' is not.**
- **Use eye contact, without staring, as a way to engage, interest and bring children back on task.**
- **Have a range of facial expression, ranging from a relaxed, open smile to a frown or shocked look.**
- **Follow the children's established routine and make it clear you know what happens and what you expect.**
- **Maintain the same expectations about behaviour as the teacher (you will have observed these very carefully).**
- **Scan the class so that you can spot (and reward) good behaviour and keep an eye out for those misbehaving or children who are off task. Developing this scanning involves looking up and around at regular intervals. It is known as teacher radar.**
- **Act purposefully. Know what you are doing and get on with it. Going straight into what you have planned engages interest and prevents disruption.**
- **Prepare interesting, relevant lessons that everyone can participate in. This is, of course, the big challenge but it is the child who is bored, left out, struggling or clueless who shows inappropriate behaviour – and becomes your nightmare.**
- **Be prepared for the unexpected. If you are ever in a situation where you do not know what to do, then do something purposeful – a few action rhymes, a bit of times tables practice, a team quiz or reading some poems can fill most gaps without undermining your authority. You should always have some emergency filler like this ready.**

These sorts of strategies make your authority and your role as the teacher clear. However, you must also be aware of the ways in which you can step out of role and lose control. Do **not**, therefore:

- Plan work they cannot do, do not understand or find boring.
- Fail to explain what you want and they should do, so that they are confused.
- Waste their time by not getting down to things at once.
- Try to use inducements or rewards in an attempt to be liked.
- Beg feebly, rather than telling: 'Will you...?' can be answered with 'No!'. 'Please...' cannot.
- Enter into arguments with children. You know best because you are the teacher – never argue with a child.
- Overpraise everything so that your praise has no meaning.
- Ignore or not recognise bad behaviour that should be dealt with.
- Use sarcasm or irony that the children cannot understand or make jokes at their expense.
- Act inconsistently or unfairly.
- Fail to distinguish yourself – children need to engage with your character through your voice and gestures: this is often what makes lessons interesting.

MINI CASE MINI CASE **MINI CASE** **MINI CASE** MINI CASE **MINI CASE** **MINI CASE**

In my first placement I was nervous. I really didn't want to seem like a know-all in front of my teacher or other students. I made the classic mistake of being too equivocal and not establishing myself as a teacher. I asked them to do things then didn't follow up if they ignored me and I couldn't get them all quiet at once. The children sussed my nerves at once and were really rowdy. I couldn't understand it at all. They were angels for Jean (the teacher) and devils for me. After a week or so Jean and my mentor sat me down and talked it through. We came up with a plan. My first aim was to get them quiet and set a simple task. I would not talk over them but I would really act, so that my voice was much more colourful. It was terrifying the first time. I had to name some naughty ones and get Jean to sit with them but I did it. I worked on using my voice, radiating authority and getting them quiet all placement. It was my hardest and most important lesson but I can honestly say it has not been an issue since

Niki, BA.

MINI CASE MINI CASE **MINI CASE** **MINI CASE** MINI CASE **MINI CASE** **MINI CASE**

I was told on my course 'Don't smile until Christmas', a humorous way of saying that you need to establish your authority before you can have a warm relationship. But it didn't stop me getting it wrong. I was too friendly and let the children in the nursery treat me differently to the other staff. They would put their hands in my pockets and do other little things that I now see were inappropriate. After a week or so I could see that I simply wasn't getting their attention like the other staff. They would ignore me and I didn't know what to do. I talked to Amy (my mentor) who helped me sort it out. It was much harder than starting out well and I struggled with establishing my authority for the whole five weeks. I didn't make the same mistake the next time.

Billie, GTP

MINI CASE MINI CASE **MINI CASE** **MINI CASE** MINI CASE **MINI CASE** **MINI CASE**

I am a lively person in real life but in class my voice just seemed to shut down. I couldn't seem to keep attention or command the children. My voice was described by a colleague I knew well as 'wimpy'. I was devastated. I did some voice training at the university and on my final placement I just went for it. I acted the whole placement, varying my voice in volume and pitch. Looking back, I feel like I was amplifying my character at the children by using my voice. I suppose that is what you need to do –

exaggerate expression and intonation so that all the children in a class are engaged. I still can't believe I was that wimpy. I am still a quiet teacher and keep a quiet class, but my voice and gestures are engaging and not boring.

Ulrika, NQT

MINI CASE MINI CASE **MINI CASE** **MINI CASE** MINI CASE **MINI CASE** **MINI CASE**

I consciously imitated my teacher on first placement. She did 'Heads, fingers, knees and toes' (a sort of action rhyme) to get the attention of the children. I did this too and it helped me establish myself. In my second placement I had an older class and used 'OK, listen' because it was the wording the teacher used to get attention. It worked well for me, although the first couple of times I had to wait quite a long time. Now I have my own class I just raise a hand in the air to get attention. It suits the calm sort of ethos I like in class. I think we all find our own style.

Rina, NQT.

Dealing with difficult behaviour

You are not the only factor in managing children's behaviour in a classroom. For very young children in the Early Years Foundation Stage, inducting children into what behaviours are and are not acceptable is a major part of the curriculum. Even if you have planned interesting content and presented it well, there will be some children whose behaviour is unacceptable some of the time and in some classes this will represent a significant challenge. You need to learn how to deal with this gradually.

At the start of your placement you must recognise that you are not alone and seek the support of the teacher. First, you need to watch your teacher carefully to identify whose behaviour is difficult and how the teacher deals with it. Some children will have recognised difficulties with their behaviour that have resulted in their being put on the SEN register. In this case they will usually have individual education plans (IEPs) that you need to look at and accommodate in your planning. Some children will also have support from a teaching assistant and behaviour support adviser. You should talk to these people and make sure you know the strategies that they find are working.

When you have identified what the teacher's expectations are, how he or she manages behaviour in class, who finds good behaviour difficult and how the teacher deals with this, you will be starting to teach sessions or lessons. It is important that you take the teacher's role to establish your authority but you do not need to do this unsupported. Ask your teacher to be on hand and discuss what you will do in a number of situations.

If a child acts inappropriately there are a number of ways you can handle the situation.

- Ignore the inappropriate behaviour – but return to discuss it later, probably in private.
- Pass it off without undue emphasis, perhaps saying something like, 'I don't think I caught that...'. This gives the offender a chance to reconsider.
- Act quickly but briefly to administer a routine warning or punishment (such as a name on the board) and move swiftly on to continue what you are doing without making the incident significant.
- Assert your authority in one way or another, perhaps by looking shocked or astonished or indicating disapproval. You should only do this where you are not going to generate a conflict you cannot win

and are not going to make the whole experience an interesting situation for the child.
- Separate the child from the others and deal privately with the issue so that the child is not performing for an audience.

If you are worried about a particular child or group of children in the class, make sure you are in control of the situation, have considered where they are sitting and with whom and, as you build confidence, ask your teacher to sit with those children or nearby. As your confidence develops you may still want to enlist the teacher to support you by identifying a point at which a child has had enough attention for bad behaviour and will be quietly put into the charge of the teacher. Even when your teacher is not in the class with you, when you are teaching confidently, you should always know where to find him or her (or someone standing in for them) and be able to send two children to get them.

When dealing with poor behaviour it is very important you are assertive in your manner and the way you discuss an incident of bad behaviour.

- Summarise the behaviour causing the problem in a simple, straightforward manner and do not allow yourself to become emotional: 'I don't like you to twirl around when we are on the mat and you must answer questions when I ask you.'
- State how you feel but do not involve other people: 'I am worried about your rudeness and I am sad that you feel you can shout out at me.'
- Describe your feelings in simple terms: 'You know our class rule is to be polite to each other at all times. Your shouting makes me feel sad because you know it is not allowed in class.'
- Empathise or show sympathy with the other person's view (without endorsing it): 'I understand that not getting a turn makes you feel upset sometimes.'
- Specify what you would like the child to do and what you will do: 'I want you to stop saying rude things and twirling around on the mat so that I can offer you a turn. I will make sure I do when I see you sitting quietly.'
- Decide what your response to the child's action will be.

Being assertive and identifying a resolution to a problem is very different from being aggressive or belligerent. You should never lose control of your temper in class. If you do, you may make a situation worse and lose authority with the children. However, it is important to be able to appear cross when necessary

Frequently asked questions

1. 'I have never taught a class of children, or even more than a small group and I know that I have to take whole classes. Suppose they simply won't do what I ask?'

If you approach the class correctly, they will do what you ask. Begin the placement by reading the behaviour policy and observing your teacher. Make absolutely sure you know the whole range of rewards and sanctions so that you can offer these appropriately. Start with a short, carefully planned activity that the children are used to doing, such as reading a story to the class. This will help you to build up your confidence gradually. The most important thing is to appear confident.

2. 'One child in my class is really trying my patience. She interrupts, shouts in class and is openly insolent. Can I send her outside to cool off?'

First of all you need to read your school policy and talk to your teacher. In general, sending children out of the class is not acceptable, as this might put them at risk. In any case, even thinking of this is very extreme and you should have exhausted the whole range of sanctions before you considered a severe measure such as this. Your school will have a procedure for dealing with poor behaviour, such a writing names on the board, keeping children in for five minutes at play and involving other staff. Explore these with the support of your teacher. Finally, remember that you are not alone on placement. To re-establish order in the class, you should ask your teacher to work with you in class and help you to manage this child.

3. 'I have a delightful nursery class. Can I give them sweets to reward good behaviour?'

It is not really a good idea to reward good behaviour with sweets for a number of reasons. The school will have a health education policy that will certainly not include the use of sweets. It would be a shame to undermine early messages about healthy eating by making sweets a reward. You may also find that some children are allergic to certain ingredients commonly found in sweets, such as lactose or nuts or nut derivatives. Finally, many parents would prefer not to have children associate sweets with rewards and to be in control of the sweets their children eat. Instead of sweets, you can use stickers and praise and take the opportunity of fruit time to enjoy eating together.

4. 'One boy in my class is blatantly rude to me and calls out in my lessons. How should I deal with it?'

First, discuss this with the teacher. Does he or she have the same problem and what action has he or she taken? You may want to ask your teacher or mentor to observe a lesson so that you can discuss the behaviour that is troubling you. You must decide, preferably with your mentor, exactly what is and is not acceptable. This will stop you over-reacting.

If the school has established practices, such as writing 'strikes' on the board and adding these up to some other punishment, use these. It is always best to use a system known to the child. You should take the child aside, so that he does not have an audience, and discuss clearly and rationally what is acceptable and unacceptable and how you will treat such behaviour. Make sure you find opportunities to praise the child for his efforts at least as often as you have to reprimand him, as this is one way to develop more acceptable behaviour.

5. 'On Friday the class was really difficult and I just lost my temper and went ballistic. Now I feel embarrassed and I am worried about controlling the class.'

Losing your temper is a sign of desperation and not something you should repeat. You need some support from your mentor or class teacher. Spend a couple of lessons observing how teachers use very small rewards and sanctions (starting with a smile or frown and working up to a sticker or name on a board) before you have a meeting with your mentor. Then review the school policy with the mentor and check you know how to reward and punish in very tiny steps. This is how to keep control of the situation. Are you using time badly, failing to explain tasks or giving children work they cannot do? Discuss this honestly with your mentor and make sure your lessons are well planned with a good pace. This will prevent trouble.

6. 'I am being driven mad by the children in my Year 4 class. Whenever I ask them to do group or individual tasks they constantly ask trivial questions about where to put

dates, what to do with rubbers and how to spell words. They don't do it to the teacher.'

There are two possibilities here. First of all, you may not be explaining the tasks clearly and failing to refer to the support systems the teacher uses. This may have left the children confused. Check you know how your teacher gives instructions and what usual practice is in terms of dates and finding spellings. Enforce these routines politely but firmly and the children will respond to routines they are used to. The second possibility is that the children have noticed that you do not know their routines and are taking advantage of the situation to put off starting work. The answer is the same – show that you know the routines.

REFLECTIVE TASK
REFLECTIVE TASK

Working with your mentor or class teacher (or even another colleague) audit the positive/negative balance of your responses to children.

Start by compiling a list of all the rewards and sanctions you use. For example:

Rewards

- Smile
- Eye contact
- 'Well done' (praise)

Sanctions

- Ignoring a comment
- Frowning at a child
- Asking someone to sit down/be quiet

Your colleagues can use this list to do a tally chart of your rewards/sanctions in a single lesson. Aim to find out:

- **What is the balance of rewards and sanctions in your lesson?**

- **Who do you give most attention to?**

- **What can you do to ensure you give more rewards than sanctions, and that this is a calm sensible reward?**

Child protection

Children and young people have a fundamental right to be protected from harm and have a right to expect schools to provide a safe and secure environment. It is a guiding principle of the law and child protection procedures that the protection and welfare of the child must always be the first priority. The protection of children and young people is a shared community responsibility and failure to provide an effective response can have serious consequences for the child. Teachers and other education staff are in a unique position to identify and help abused children. Your school will have a child protection policy that you should read.

In a school placement, if you suspect any child is subject to the categories of abuse identified by the DfES (2004) *Safeguarding Children in Education* – neglect, physical injury, sexual abuse or emotional abuse, or a child discloses abuse to you, you must follow the school policy and inform the teacher designated responsible (who will be identified in the school policy). This is a highly confidential matter and you should treat it as such. The teacher responsible may choose to share the information with the class teacher but it is not a matter for you to discuss with other staff.

If a child chooses to disclose abuse to you, you should:

- listen to them quietly in privacy but do not interrogate them or ask leading questions;
- make it clear to the child that you cannot keep the information confidential;
- be calm, reassuring and non-judgemental and do not seem to reproach the child, i.e. avoid questions like 'Why didn't you tell...?'
- make a record of what the child has said as soon as you can and date it;
- tell the designated teacher for child protection, preferably on the day the disclosure happens, and pass your notes to him or her.

You can be sure that any allegation of this sort will be dealt with sensitively, swiftly and thoroughly. You may need support yourself to cope with this sort of experience. In the first instance you can get this from your mentor, course tutor or a university counsellor. You can also ring the NSPCC helpline on 0808 800 5000.

A SUMMARY OF **KEY POINTS**

> On professional placement you will work with a range of other adults, including other practitioners, teaching assistants, parents, visiting professionals and administrative staff.
> Working closely with other practitioners and teaching assistants involves understanding their roles and planning carefully for their involvement in all parts of the lesson or session.
> Managing the behaviour of the children you are teaching involves signalling clearly that you are the teacher, know what you are doing, have interesting work and high expectations. Sometimes, this is not as simple as it sounds.
> To take the place of the regular teacher you need to know how the school, class and teacher work. Read the school policy, observe the class and the teacher. Make sure that you know the very fine grading of rewards and sanctions and the teacher's expectations for behaviour.
> Act the part of the teacher. Your body language, how you speak to the children and your apparent confidence, together with well-paced lessons and appropriate activities, will work to ensure an orderly learning environment.
> Your teacher is there to support you. As you gain confidence you will take over managing behaviour in class but you should not be afraid to work closely with the teacher to address particular issues.
> Read the school child protection policy and know who the designated teacher responsible is. If you have any child protection concerns, report to the designated teacher and follow it up with a written, dated report.

Resources

The government teacher advice website has very useful materials on all the issues in this chapter, including behaviour management, child protection and working with other adults in school: **www.teachernet.gov.uk**.

The TDA fund an ITT Professional Resource Network about behaviour management that contains many useful articles and examples of guidance: **www.behaviour4learning.ac.uk**.

NSPCC helpline: tel 0808 800 5000.

DfES (2004) *Safeguarding Children in Education*, DfES/0027/2004.

The Protection of Children Act, HMSO, 1999.

8
Moving on

This chapter offers advice about completion of placements. By the end of the chapter you will know how to:

- **conclude your placement;**
- **review your progress on placement;**
- **prepare for the next placement or your NQT year;**
- **begin to look for a teaching job.**

Concluding a placement

The end of the placement is an important time for you. It is a goal you have worked hard to achieve but it is also slightly strange for you to be passing the class back to another teacher. A report of some kind about your assessment will be written by your mentor and/or class teacher and you will discuss with them how well you have achieved your targets. You will also be concluding some important relationships. The first of these is the relationship with your class teacher, who will be used to working closely with you and will have to take up the reins of a class who have become used to you. As your placement may end before the end of a term, your teacher may need to carry on teaching seamlessly when you leave. In the last week of your placement you need to make sure you do the following things:

- **Return all the resources you have borrowed. It is very annoying for your teacher to find, a week after you have left, that you have mistakenly retained photocopiable sheets, or computer software.**
- **Check that you have taken all your resources and equipment away, as it will inconvenience everyone if you have to keep coming back.**
- **Mark and record all the work children have done for you. If there are pieces for assessment, levelling or Foundation Stage profile contributions, ensure these are filed in the right place and correctly annotated.**
- **Have a final tidy up and check that all books and resources are in the teacher's allocated places.**
- **Ensure you pass up-to-date records of the work the children have done with you to your teacher. It is a good idea to arrange a time to discuss the records and to highlight the objectives the children have addressed on the medium-term plan. This, with your records, allows the teacher to take over again smoothly.**
- **Check any outstanding commitments. If you have agreed to come back to help with an assembly or a trip, make sure you know the details before you leave. If you are coming back for another placement later, mention this to your teacher.**

Most importantly of all, make sure you thank your teacher explicitly for his or her help and the training they have given you, even if you are coming back to the school or class for a further placement. Make sure you make this more than a casual leave-taking: pick out some specific help they have given you and something you have learned from them. Most trainees follow up thanks with a short note or card. The teacher has given you a great deal of support and entrusted their class to you. It is rewarding for him or her to be reminded that you are grateful for this when they are engaged in the hard work of rebuilding their relationship with the class.

Possibly the most important training relationship you have in school is with your mentor. The formal conclusion to a placement will be a discussion about your progress during the placement and this will contribute to a report or profile that assesses your performance against the Standards for QTS. You will look at a draft of your report or the evidence that will contribute to your report. If you are leaving the school, even if you are coming back at a later date, you need to conclude your relationship with your mentor.

- **Return all the resources you have borrowed from your mentor, other staff, the resources room or staffroom.**
- **Check that any displays you are responsible for are complete and labelled.**
- **Check any outstanding commitments and that you have a copy of your report from your mentor.**

Thank your mentor explicitly for the training they have given you. Your mentor may not have taught alongside you every day, like your teacher, but they have made a big contribution to your training. As with your teacher, explicit thanks and a short note are thoughtful gestures.

You may also want to ask your mentor, or head teacher, for a reference. If this is your final placement you may want a reference quite soon (or even during the placement). If this is not your final placement you may still want to have a second or third reference from the mentor or head teacher for a future application for a teaching post. You may also want to ask for references for vacation work or non-teaching posts. When you ask for a reference be explicit.

- **Ask if the mentor or head teacher is prepared to offer you a reference. In most cases a reference is offered gladly. Professionals will not write a bad reference for anyone. They usually simply say they would prefer not to offer a reference. Mentors and head teachers will never decline to offer a reference simply because they do not want the effort.**
- **Who would your mentor prefer to be named – the mentor him or herself or the head teacher? Check that you know the full name, title and professional position of your mentor or head – it is surprising how often trainees do not get this right.**
- **Say when you expect to be applying for jobs and whether these will be exclusively teaching jobs or will include things like vacation jobs or voluntary work.**
- **Be clear about anything you would like your referee to mention (such as participation in out-of-school events) or avoid mentioning, such as a disability or illness.**
- **Make sure that the mentor or head has your contact details and that you have theirs. You should contact them to let them know when you use their name as a referee in any application.**
- **Always thank your head teacher at the end of a placement, if you are leaving that school. The head teacher has opened up the school to you and made you welcome.**

Finally, when you finish a placement, you need to conclude your relationship with the class. It will have been a very complex, intense and demanding relationship and leaving the children can make you feel very emotional. The children in your placement class have played a big part in your training and you will remember some of them for the rest of your career. You have some responsibilities towards them as well. You need to make sure you have returned their work and kept any promises you made to them in terms of rewards such as 'Golden Time', exciting activities or games.

The end of the placement is not the time for a sentimental speech, no matter how emotional you feel, but do make sure you explain to the class that you will be leaving them. You should explain this positively so that they understand that this is something you had planned and that you have enjoyed your time with them. Pick out some incidents or lessons you have particularly enjoyed and some examples of good classwork or behaviour. You should also make it clear who will be teaching them now. You might want to put up a poster or card to thank the children for the time you've had as their teacher.

After leaving a school you have a duty of confidentiality towards the school, teachers and children. If you use examples of school documents in assignments, you should ask the permission of the school and make sure that the extract is anonymised. You should not gossip about the schools, the teachers or the children and if you do use examples of your experience, or children's work, in the professional setting of your course you should do so in such a way that the teachers, school or children involved cannot be identified. This is also important where photos of the school or children have been taken, with the permission of the school.

Reviewing your progress on placement

You will review your progress as you go through your placement but there is a key review point towards the end of a placement. There are a number of reasons for this:

- **to check you have done all the tasks you planned and used all the training opportunities on offer;**
- **to review whether you have met targets you set for the placement or during the placement;**
- **to identify progress you have made towards demonstrating the Standards for QTS;**
- **to decide what constitutes evidence of your progress towards the Standards for QTS and to store this appropriately;**
- **to prepare for a review meeting with your mentor or course tutor;**
- **to prepare a portfolio of work in preparation for a job interview;**
- **to set new targets for future placements, study of particular areas or your NQT year.**

It is important for you to review your targets and progress before the last week of the placement so that you can identify what progress you have made and the evidence for this. In this way you can be prepared for a meeting with your mentor to discuss your final report. You will be assessed by the mentor and possibly a course tutor but you will have the opportunity to present evidence for your assessment by discussion and referring to your files. You do not have the right to alter their assessment but your mentor will want to make sure your report does justice to your performance against the standards for QTS and will consider all the evidence. In this way you can contribute positively to your assessment.

The Career Entry and Development Profile

Your placement report will summarise your achievements and identify areas for further work. These can be turned into targets for your next placement or used to complete transition point 1 in the Career Entry and Development Profile (CEDP). The profile is a document you use to guide the process of reflection and review as you complete your initial teacher training and go through your induction year. The profile document suggests prompt questions that can be asked at the three key transition points:

- **the end of ITT (transition point 1);**
- **the beginning of your NQT year (transition point 2);**
- **the end of your NQT year (transition point 3).**

The CEDP helps you to:

- build on your achievements and identify your professional development needs;
- make links between your ITT, induction and continuing professional development;
- prepare for meetings with your tutors and induction tutor;
- set your current priorities in the wider context of career and professional development.

The CEDP helps your ITT provider to prepare you to play an active role in your induction period.

The CEDP is prepared annually by the TDA and will be given to you by your ITT provider near to the end of your training. It is also available as a package of online materials. The web pages at **www.tda.gov.uk/cedp** provide information on the CEDP and induction in general. On this site you will find descriptions of the processes that you will be undertaking at each of the three transition points. The online materials have interactive elements and sample formats for recording your responses, setting objectives, and writing action plans.

As you come to the end of your ITT programme, you will want to think about how far you have come in your professional development. Your ITT provider will also be preparing you for your induction period and helping you to understand your own role in that process.

The transition point 1 section of the CEDP will help you to think about your experience before, during and beyond your formal training programme, including your placements, and to identify your key achievements and aspirations in relation to teaching.

You should aim to use the CEDP to set targets that:

- reflect and build on the strengths in your practice;
- develop aspects of the teacher's role in which you are particularly interested;
- provide more experience, or build up your expertise, in areas where you have developed to a more limited extent so far.

At transition point 1, the CEDP poses focus questions that you should reflect on. You are not expected to write lengthy answers to each question. The processes of reflection and professional discussion with your course tutor or mentor are more important and these will be reflected in the notes you make.

- At this stage, which aspect(s) of teaching do you find most interesting and rewarding?
- What has led to your interest in these areas?
- How would you like to develop these interests?
- As you approach the award of QTS, what do you consider to be your main strengths and achievements as a teacher?
- Why do you think this?
- What examples do you have of your achievements in these areas?
- In which aspects of teaching would you value further experience in the future? For example:
  - aspects of teaching about which you feel less confident, or where you have had
  - limited opportunities to gain experience;
  - areas of particular strength or interest on which you want to build further.
- At the moment, which of these areas do you particularly hope to develop during your induction period?

As you look ahead to your career in teaching, you may be thinking about your longer-term professional aspirations and goals. Do you have any thoughts at this stage about how you would like to see your career develop?

Note down your response to the questions, where you might find evidence to support your thinking, and/or the reasoning that led you to this response. You will want to draw on evidence that is already available, for example:

- **reports on your teaching during your placements;**
- **observation reports written by your mentor, class teacher or course tutor;**
- **examples of your planning for placement;**
- **records of targets and objectives set during your ITT programme;**
- **your own audits of your progress towards the standards for QTS;**
- **course assignments or subject audits.**

You will want to be able to find this evidence and, if necessary, share it with others, like your tutors. You may wish to copy your notes, to include them in other professional development records or portfolios, or share them with others, for example, to prepare for further discussions with your tutors or mentors. It is for you and your tutor to decide on how the profile can be used in the most supportive way.

Your ITT tutor should sign to confirm that your transition point 1 discussion took place. A form for them to sign is included in the CEDP at transition point 1. The CEDP is a mandatory part of ITT. It enables your school to:

- **understand your strengths and experiences by the end of ITT;**
- **support your professional development through your NQT year;**
- **support constructive dialogue between NQTs and induction tutors;**
- **make links between induction, continuing professional development and performance management.**

Induction for newly qualified teachers

If you are completing your final placement, you will probably be looking forward to getting a job in teaching and becoming an NQT. Induction for newly qualified teachers is compulsory, follows ITT and is the foundation for continuing professional development throughout your career. The induction period must be undertaken by NQTs who wish to work in maintained schools and non-maintained special schools. The induction period may also be done while working in independent schools but not all of them offer this. Check when you apply for jobs, as failure to do a recognised induction will mean you do not gain QTS.

During the induction period you have to demonstrate you have continued to meet the standards for QTS, and met all the induction standards. You will have an individualised programme of support from a designated induction tutor during your induction year. This includes observation of the your teaching, watching more experienced teachers in different settings, and a professional review of progress at least every half term. You will not teach more than 90 per cent of a normal timetable during the period, to allow your induction to take place.

The head teacher is responsible with appropriate bodies (the LA or the Independent Schools Council Teacher Induction Panel) and will make a final recommendation as to whether you have passed or failed your induction period. The appropriate body makes the final decision, and there is a right of appeal to the General Teaching Council for England (GTCE). The DfES guidance on induction, *The Induction Support Programme for Newly Qualified Teachers*, is now available online.

Applying for a teaching job

During your teaching placement you may start to apply for jobs. This will affect your placement in a number of ways:

- **you will need time off for visits and interviews;**
- **you will want to use your placement experience positively in your application;**
- **you will want to ask for references and ensure your referees are clear about what is required.**

Time off for visits and interviews

Jobs are usually advertised by individual schools or NQT pools, a group of schools recruiting together. You must make sure you check the systems in place in your target areas – it is not uncommon for schools to advertise individually and also be part of an education authority pool. When you respond to an advertisement the school or education authority will send you an information pack and details of how to apply for the job. Your ITT provider will also give you information.

When you are considering applying for a job you may be invited to look around the school or you may ask to do so. This could present problems because of the time taken out of your placement, especially if you are applying for a job at some distance from your placement school. There is no doubt that an informal visit can be useful to you and some schools schedule specific times to take a large number of applicants around the school together. However, you must consider the impact of absence from school on your training. If you applied for six jobs, visited all the schools and went for interviews at each one, you would miss at least a week of placement – two weeks if the schools you are applying to are not very close to the placement school. As you have to complete a certain amount of placement time in a school and take sustained responsibility for a class on final placement, a large number of visits could affect the outcome of your placement. It may be better to try to visit schools after the end of the school day, or to explain to schools that your placement commitments prevent you from visiting informally. You will almost always be given a tour of the school prior to interview and will have the opportunity to withdraw from the interview after this if you do not think the school would suit you.

If you have applied for a post and are invited to interview, you should ask your mentor for permission to attend: this will involve missing school placement that day. In practice this is a courtesy and you will always be given permission to attend interviews. Mentors and teachers will help you to prepare your application and you should discuss a draft of your letter of application, supporting statement or CV (whatever is requested) with your mentor, if possible. It is also a good idea to ask your mentor or class teacher to help you to prepare for interview. Preparation might take a number of forms:

- **Discussion of hot topics in the educational press or recent initiatives in school is always useful. Discussing these issues with a teacher will help you to explore the issues from another perspective. Consider what the effects of new ideas are for teachers, schools and children.**

- Role playing a mock interview with the mentor, teacher or another member of school staff can help you to conquer nerves and prepare your interview manner.
- Asking your teacher to help you to plan any teaching you are required to do as part of your interview. It is not uncommon to be asked to teach something to the class. Although you will not be able to prepare a perfect lesson because you do not know the children, you can still show that you know the relevant curricula, have good ideas, know a range of teaching strategies, are aware of a range of resources and have a good manner with the children. Your teacher or mentor may be able to spot obvious *faux pas* or overambitious plans if you ask to discuss them.

If you apply for a job through a teaching pool you will usually go for an interview for the pool first and may then be invited to look around schools that have jobs available. This is a different sort of school visit from the informal pre-interview visit because you will be looking at a school to see whether you would take a job there. You should go on these visits but be aware of the time you will lose on your placement.

Using your placement experience in your application for a teaching post

You will be given support in applying for a teaching post elsewhere in your ITT programme but it is important that your application includes insights from your placement because this will show that you have learnt from your experiences.

When you write in response to an advertisement for a teaching post or for details of an NQT pool you will receive a specification for the job (see Figure 8.1). This may be general, like the sample below, or there may be very specific requirements associated with a school. As an NQT, you cannot become a curriculum co-ordinator in your NQT year.

There are two main types of written application for Primary and Early Years teaching posts:

- the LA or school application form, which usually includes a personal statement or letter of application;
- your own CV and letter of application.

The information pack you receive from the school or LA will tell you what is required.

Complete application forms neatly and accurately, in a way that will demonstrate enthusiasm. The usual rules for form filling apply: read the instructions carefully and follow them. Write a draft first (and keep it for future reference); do not leave gaps – write N/A if appropriate; check all your dates and have all your information to hand; make sure your writing is neat and everything is correctly spelled and make sure your personal statement (or letter) is effective. Allow plenty of time to fill in your application – it takes longer than you think – and make sure you have done a thorough review of your placement and your record of professional development or training plan.

You will be required to write either a supporting statement or letter of application as part of the form or a supporting letter. The first thing you should do to prepare this is to examine thoroughly the specification and/or job description to work out what the school or LA is looking for. Then read the instructions for completing the form very carefully. Filling out this form is a chore but it is your chance to market your skills. Do not be too modest nor make

Newly Qualified Teacher Specification
Experience .... (Appropriate teaching practice experience.) ....
Qualifications .... (QTS or the ability to achieve this under current DfES regulations.) ....
Knowledge and aptitudes.. ....
Knowledge and understanding of the NC requirements for the relevant age range. ....
Ability to plan deliver, monitor and evaluate children's learning... ....
Knowledge and understanding of the principles of assessment and record keeping and their use to promote the educational and personal development of the pupils. ....
Ability to communicate ideas clearly to a variety of groups. ....
Understanding of the requirements of children with special educational needs. ....
Ability to effectively manage and motivate children. ....
Ability to work as part of a team and to develop positive relationships with pupils, colleagues, parents and where appropriate, outside agencies.. ....
Ability to demonstrate a commitment to equality of opportunity for all pupils....................................... ....
Ability to demonstrate a commitment to high educational standards and to maximising the achievement of all pupils.. ....
Ability to demonstrate a commitment to continuing professional development...................................... ....

Figure 8.1. Sample teaching job specification

exaggerated claims. You may find the completed form slightly embarrassing, because it spells out your achievements and qualities, but it should not be untruthful.

There are many ways of writing your letter of application or supporting statement but the following points should be considered.

- **Say why you are applying for this post in particular. Include any local links, faith issues or visits to the school.**
- **Give a brief overview of your training (but do not repeat everything you have put in the application form). Also mention your degree (PGCE or GTP) and any relevant projects or experiences.**
- **Reference to your formal school placements including:**
  - **when you did the placement;**
  - **what years you have taught;**
  - **the level of responsibility you took.**
- **Special features of the placement such as open plan schools or team teaching.**
- **Examples of how you plan, teach, monitor and evaluate learning outcomes, behaviour management strategies, work with parents, etc.**
- **Write a little about your vision or beliefs for Early Years or Primary education and the principles that underpin your practice. This might be how children learn, classroom management, teaching styles, etc. This gives the school a flavour of what you are like as a teacher.**
- **Details of your personal experiences: leisure interests or involvement with children. Make these relevant to your work a teacher.**

One of the easier ways to organise this information is to identify a number of subheadings taken from the specification or job description such as:

- **teaching experience (placements);**
- **commitment to teaching;**
- **knowledge, skills and aptitudes;**
- **planning and organisation;**
- **strengths and interests;**
- **personal qualities.**

Organise your information under these headings. You can then remove your subheadings and have a well-organised letter to discuss with your mentor, teacher or careers adviser.

Write a letter of application, of not more than two sides of A4, setting out your experience, knowledge, skills and aptitudes and views about education. Discuss this general draft with your mentor or teacher and ask them to tell you about the impact and the impression it makes.

You may find yourself writing a *curriculum vitae* (CV) for the first time for a job application during your placement. Your CV sets out the important information about you, usually on no more than two sides of A4. Make sure you have some good quality, white paper to print on.

If you are basing your CV on a version you have used before, do not just churn it out for job after job. Check first that it matches the specification for each individual job.

PRACTICAL TASK PRACTICAL TASK **PRACTICAL TASK** PRACTICAL TASK **PRACTICAL TASK**

Use the specification in Figure 8.1 to review your experience, qualifications and knowledge, skills and aptitudes. Go through each point asking yourself:

- **What evidence do I have that I meet this criterion?**
- **What have I learned about this on my placement?**
- **What else do I need to be able to do to achieve this?**

Finally, ask yourself what you want to focus on in your continuing professional development during the induction year.

Things you can leave out of a CV

- There is no need to include your date of birth, age, marital status or ethnic origin.
- A photograph is not necessary for teaching CVs and can trigger subconscious prejudice.
- Do not include your reasons for changing jobs. Keep your CV factual: where you worked and when.
- Do not include failures on your CV. Keep it focused on what you have achieved.
- Do not include salary information.

Things to include on your CV

- Contact details. Make sure that contact details you give will really reach you: if you have an e-mail address that you rarely check, do not include it. Ideally, include your postal address, any telephone numbers you have (landline and mobile) and your e-mail address if you will be checking it frequently.
- Your gender, if it is not obvious from your name.
- A short skills summary or supporting statement (see below).
- Your education. This is best organised as follows: primary, secondary, further, higher.
- Your qualifications, listed with the most recent first, including results.
- Your work experience and placement experiences – most recent first (any positions you held more than about ten years ago can be left out).
- Interests – only real and genuine ones, e.g. any sports you actively participate in. If these hobbies and interests can convey a sense of your personality, all the better. Include any non-teaching qualifications that may have arisen from your hobbies or interests here as well.
- Membership of professional associations (not unions).
- Nationality, National Insurance number and referee details (or a sentence to say, 'Referees available on request') can be included at the end of your CV.

A skills summary need only be around 200 words, but you can still cover a lot of ground.

- Write in the first person.
- Every word must be relevant and grammar should be immaculate.
- Use interesting adverbs and adjectives to lift the text.
- Do not just focus on experience. Achievements, accountability and competence are more important.
- Aim to give a sense of your creativity, personal management and integrity: the reader will want to see that you have strong communication skills and are perhaps even leadership material.
- Some people prefer to include a short bulleted list of around six key skills.

Suggested layout

- When designing your CV, you need to be economical with space. While the page should not look cluttered, excess space will look messy and ill thought-out.
- Present your contact details across the top of the first page (like a letterhead) to preserve space.
- Use a clear, standard font such as Times New Roman or Arial.
- Avoid abbreviations unless they are universally understood.
- If you really cannot fit everything on to two sides of A4, try reducing the font size slightly. This will mean the print is still large enough to read, but will give you a little more room to play with. Avoid lines of just one or two words, as this is a waste of space.
- When you have designed your CV on screen, print off a draft version and try to view it through fresh eyes. Is it likely to grab the attention of a reader within a few seconds? Is it visually pleasing? Are there any errors? It is a good idea to ask someone else to cast an eye over it as it is easy to miss typographical errors on documents you have been working on yourself.
- Be aware that this is not a one-off task. Once you have completed your CV, you will need to keep it up to date.

A sample CV is shown in Figure 8.2.

Asking for references

You will usually be asked to supply the names, positions and contact details of two referees. The first should be a senior member of staff of your ITT provider. Check carefully who this should be. It is common for universities to use the name of the head of department, even though your tutor will write the reference. It is essential to get this name right for two reasons. If you do not get a first reference from your ITT provider the job advertiser will usually assume you have something to hide. Secondly, the reference system in a large ITT provider will be geared up to a swift response but it will only work if you get the right name. The wrong name will slow down your reference and may put you at a disadvantage. Your second referee should usually be from your placement school.

Interview portfolios

As a trainee you will be maintaining a training plan or record of professional development that contains evidence to demonstrate your achievement of the standards. This will contain placement assessment reports, observation notes, written assignments, mentor meeting notes and other evidence.

You may be asked to take this training plan or record with you to interview. Even if you are not asked to bring a portfolio you may want to do so. You can offer this to your interviewers – they do not have to spend much time looking at it but it does indicate you are well prepared and professional.

An interview portfolio can be a substantial document but, more usually, is a slim document containing some of the following:

- title and content page, preferably with a photo of you teaching happily on it;
- concise CV;
- placement assessment reports (one or more);
- a really good lesson plan or two, some examples of the work associated with the lesson and the lesson evaluation;

<u>Emily Jones</u>
529 Highgate Road, Reading, Berkshire RG1 2AB
Telephone: 0128 678 3567, mobile: 07887 987654, e-mail: EMMY00@aol.com

I am a Newly Qualified Teacher trained to teach mathematics to the 3–8 age group. My previous work experience as an accountant in the City enabled me to develop an understanding of management in a large multinational corporation as well as demonstrable communication skills. Part of my role was the delivery of internal training for new staff. During my initial teacher training I taught in an inner-city nursery and the Early Years Foundation Stage unit of a school with a large multi-racial population. In addition to my teaching I developed a successful everyday mathematics after-school workshop for parents that crossed age and race boundaries and was recognised by the head and governors as a constructive addition to the wider school culture.

Education
Primary: 1982–1988 St John's Primary School, Reading
Secondary: 1988–1993 Reading High School for Girls, Reading
Further: 1993–1995 The Abbey Sixth Form College, Wokingham
Higher: 1995–1998 University of Warwick BA
1998–2004 Membership of the Society of Chartered Accountants
2004–2005 Institute of Education, University of London PGCE

Qualifications
PGCE: Early Years
Degree: mathematics and statistics 2.1
A–levels: mathematics A, statistics A, physics B, general studies B
GCSEs: mathematics A, English literature A, English language B, physics B, history A, ICT A, art B, geography B, French A, biology B

Professional development
During my initial teacher training I completed an LEA-run First Aid in the Classroom course and attended a 'Developing Storysacks' training day.

Work Experience
2002–2003 ITT placements: Grove School Nursery, Camden and Nelson Mandela Primary School, Westminster
1998–2002 British International Bank, London, Accountant
1995–1998 Vacation positions with Marks and Spencer and Waterstone's, Reading

Interests
I have run a local Brownies group for some years. I also run to keep fit and have completed the London marathon.

Additional qualifications
Full, clean driving licence.
Berkshire County Junior Football Coaching

Nationality
British

National Insurance Number
TY 123456B
Referees available on request

Figure 8.2. Sample CV

- a mentor, tutor or class teacher observation of a lesson;
- a sample mentor meeting summary;
- an example of a piece of written work (and the marking sheet) if relevant;
- a few photos of you teaching. Choose these carefully as you really want to present a specific image. Generally you might choose one photo of you teaching a large group or class, one of you looking sensitive with a group and, ideally, one of you teaching elsewhere – pond dipping is ideal. Remember, choose photos to suit a particular job. If the school is very ICT conscious, make sure there is a picture with you using ICT. If the school is keen to improve its physical education, a photo of your tag rugby lesson would be ideal. Make sure you follow your placement school's policy on photograph use and that the school and children are not identifiable.
- One or two photographs of displays, school visits you have been on, after school clubs or assemblies you have done.
- Any evidence of your special interest – coaching certificates, first aid, cookery, etc.

In practice, trainees tell us that interview panels do not spend much time on interview portfolios and usually just flick through the content. However, by preparing this you not only demonstrate professionalism but also have the chance to present a tailored image of your achievements to the panel in addition to your written application.

Resources

The Career Entry and Development Profile and support materials are available at: **www.tda.gov.uk/cedp**.

The Induction Support Programme for Newly Qualified Teachers (Reference: DfES/0458/2003), is now available at **www.tda.gov.uk/induction**. This site also provides detailed guidance about induction.

Detailed information about applying for a teaching post is available from the Association of Graduate Careers Advisory Services in the publication: AGCAS (2005) *Getting a Teaching Job in Schools: A guide to finding your first appointment*.

Most school vacancies are advertised in the *Times Educational Supplement* (Fridays) **www.tesjobs.co.uk**.

The *Guardian* (Tuesdays) **www.jobsunlimited.co.uk**.

The *Daily Telegraph* (Independent Schools) **www.telegraph.co.uk**.

The *Independent* (Thursdays) **www.independent.co.uk**.

Some of these operate an electronic job alert system.

For general information about teaching in the private sector:

Independent Schools Council Information Service (ISCIS) at **www.iscis.uk.net**.

Incorporated Association of Preparatory Schools (IAPS) at **www.iaps.co.uk**.

Your union is an excellent source of help, advice and support in applying for a teaching post:

www.teachersunion.org.uk (NASUWT).

www.data.teachers.org.uk (NUT).

www.askatl.org.uk (ATL).

Other useful online resources for finding a teaching post are available at:

www.eteach.com.

www.teachernet.gov.uk.

www.prospects.ac.uk.

Make sure you use you local or university careers service.

GTC(E) or (GTC(W). **www.gtce.org.uk/ www.gtcw.org.uk/**. The General Teaching Council for England and General Teaching Council for Wales exist to hold a register of all teachers (who are not barred from teaching). You should join this. Details are available online.

Glossary

ATL Association of Teachers and Lecturers. For further details see www.askatl.org.uk/

ATP Approved Training Provider. For further details see www.dfes.gov.uk/providersregister/

BA with QTS Bachelor of arts with qualified teacher status. A degree in an arts or humanities-based subject which also leads to qualified teacher status.

BEd with QTS Bachelor of education with qualified teacher. status A degree in education which also leads to qualified teacher status.

BSc with QTS Bachelor of science with qualified teacher status. A degree in a science-based subject which also leads to qualified teacher status.

Class teacher A teacher of the class with which you do most of your work during a placement.

CPD Continuing professional development. For further details see www.teachernet/gov/uk/professionaldevelopment/

DfES Department for Education and Skills. The English government department which creates policy. For further details see www.dfes.gov.uk/

EAL English as an additional language.

Extended school A school that provides a range of services and activities often beyond the school day to help meet the needs of its pupils, their families and the wider community. For more information see www.qca.org.uk/10013.html

Foundation stage The earliest years of schooling for UK children (ages 3–5 years). For more information see www.qca.org.uk/160.html

GTP Graduate Teacher Programme. An employment teacher training programme for graduates. For further details see www.tda.gov.uk/Recruit/thetrainingprocess/typesofcourse/gtp.aspx

GTCE General Teaching Council for England and GTCW General Teaching Council for Wales. The GTC is the professional body for teaching in England and Wales whose purpose is to help improve standards of teaching and the quality of learning in the public interest. www.gtce.org.uk or www.gtcw.org.uk

HEI Higher education institution. A university, school or college offering degree-level and postgraduate education.

Humanities A collective term for a range of subjects including: history, geography, religious studies, sociology and others.

ICT Information and communications technology. For more information see www.becta.org.uk/

Induction period Following recommendation for the award of QTS you are required to undertake a successful period of induction. You set targets for this at the end of ITT and have induction standards to meet. For more information see www.tda/gov.uk/teachers/induction.aspx

Inset In-service education and training. Training for qualified teachers.

ITT Initial teacher training. Course of training that leads to qualified teacher status (QTS). For further information see www.tda.gov/uk/

ITT provider A school, college or university that offers initial teacher training courses. For more information see www.tda.gov/uk/partners/funding/accreditation/ittproviders.aspx

Key Stages The different stages of compulsory schooling in the UK. The teacher training you receive will be provided according to the needs of the key stages you intend to teach. If you are training to teach primary or Early Years, you will usually train for two Key Stages, but need to know about those above and below. Some courses will train teachers for KS2 and KS3, crossing the usual age at which children move between primary and secondary schools.

Foundation Key Stage Children aged 3–5 or EYFS Children aged birth to 5.

KS1 Key Stage 1. First stage of compulsory schooling for UK children (ages 5–7 years).

KS2 Key Stage 2. Second stage of compulsory schooling for UK children (ages 7–11 years).

KS3 Key Stage 3. Third stage of compulsory schooling for UK children (ages 12–13 years).

KS4 Key Stage 4. Fourth stage of compulsory schooling for UK children (ages 14–16 years).

LEA Local education authority. These organisations provide services for schools in their area.

LSA Learning support assistant.

Maintained school A school that is maintained by the state.

Mentor The person in school who manages your placement offering advice, support and, usually, assessing your progress. The details of the role of your mentor will be in your course information.

MFL Modern foreign languages. French, Spanish, German, Gujarati, etc. The government is committed to introducing MFL for all primary pupils by 2010. For further details see www.qca.org.uk/10076_10943.html

Middle school A middle school has pupils from KS2 and KS3. Depending on the age balance of those pupils the school can be deemed primary or secondary.

MPS Main Pay Scale. Determines classroom teachers' basic salaries. There are now two scales: one for England and Wales and one for inner London. For further details consult your union.

NASUWT National Union of Schoolmasters Union of Women Teachers. For further details see www.nasuwt.org.uk/

NC National Curriculum. Covers what pupils should be taught in state-maintained schools. The National Curriculum embraces 12 subjects overall, and is divided into four Key Stages according to age. Available online at www.curriculumonline.gov.uk/

NQT Newly qualified teacher. A teacher who has just been recommended for qualified teacher status and who needs to complete an induction period to confirm the award. For more information see www.tda.gov.uk/teachers/induction.aspx

NUT National Union of Teachers. For more information, see www.teachers.org.uk/

Ofsted Office for Standards in Education. The body responsible for inspection in schools and teacher training. See www.ofsted.gov.uk/

OTTP Overseas trained teacher programme. An individually tailored programme of training and assessment enabling OTTs to achieve qualified teacher status in England. For more information, see www.tda.gov/uk/Recruit/thetrainingprocess/typesofcourse/ottp.aspx

PE Physical education.

PGCE Postgraduate Certificate of Education. A teacher training qualification which may be at Postgraduate (Master's) level or at Undergraduate (H) level, in which case it may be referred to as a Professional Certificate.

Profile report This is the document completed at the end of your placement which sets out your progress towards meeting the Standards for QTS and your targets for future work. It may have another name (report, assessment, etc.). It will form part of your training record.

PSHE Personal, social and health education.

PTA Parent-teacher association. For general information see www.ncpta.org.uk/

QCA Qualifications and Curriculum Authority. See www.qca.org.uk/

QTS Qualified Teacher Status. The status trainee teachers achieve; recommendation for this by meeting all of the required Standards. It is confirmed after a period of induction. You must have this qualification to teach in a state-maintained school. For more information, see www.tda.gov.uk/Recruit/becomingateacher/qualifiedteacherstatus.aspx

RB Recommending body. A school, local education authority, higher education institution or any other body that can organise an appropriate teaching training plan.

RTP Registered Teacher Programme. An employment-based teacher training programme. See www.tda.gov.uk/Recruit/thetrainingprocess/typesofcourse/rtp.aspx

SCITT School-centred initial teacher training. Teacher training provided by schools in partnership with higher education institutions and local education authorities. For general information, see www.tda.gov.uk/Recruit/thetrainingprocess/typesofcourse/scitt.aspx

Schools in special measures Schools deemed by Her Majesty's Chief Inspector of Schools to be failing to provide an acceptable standard of education for its pupils.

SEN Special educational needs. For some information see www.direct/gov/uk/en/EducationAndLearning/Schools/SpecialEducationalNeeds/index.htm

SENCO SEN coordinator. The teacher in school with responsibility for the delivery of services for children with special educational needs.

Standards for the award of QTS These are the standards you have to achieve to be recommended for the award of QTS at the end of your ITT. See www.tda.gov.uk/partners/ittstandards

TA Teaching assistant.

TES *Times Educational Supplement*. A good source of information about teaching job vacancies. See www.tes.co.uk/

TDA Training and Development Agency for Schools. Formerly the Teacher Training Agency. This is the place to find full information about rules, regulations, induction, etc. www.tda.gov.uk/

Training record or **training plan** This is a document which summarises your progress towards the standards for QTS and the targets you still need to meet. It usually starts with information about your experience and skills before ITT and is created by adding information about your progress, such as audits of subject knowledge, assignment feedback, placement profiles, etc. The final document will be your Induction Profile, which sets out your training targets for the Induction period.

Voluntary aided schools Schools in England and Wales, maintained by the LEA, for which a foundation (generally religious) appoints most of the governing body.

Voluntary controlled schools Schools in England and Wales, maintained by the LEA, for which a foundation (generally religious) appoints some – but not most – of the governing body.

Year 1 to Year 13 The way year groups are divided in English schools, from nursery through to sixth form:
- **Reception year: 4/5-year-olds;**
- **Year 1: 5/6-year-olds;**
- **Year 2: 6/7-year-olds;**
- **Year 3: 7/8-year-olds;**
- **Year 4: 8/9-year-olds;**
- **Year 5: 9/10-year-olds;**
- **Year 6: 10/11-year-olds;**
- **Year 7: 11/12-year-olds**
- **Year 8: 12/13-year-olds;**
- **Year 9: 13/14-year-olds;**
- **Year 10: 14/15-year-olds;**
- **Year 11: 15/16-year-olds;**
- **Year 12: 16/17-year-olds;**
- **Year 13: 17/18-year-olds.**

Index

Achieving QTS

The Achieving QTS series continues to grow with nearly 50 titles in 8 separate strands. Our titles address issues of teaching and learning across both primary and secondary phases in a highly practical and accessible manner, making each title an invaluable resource for trainee teachers.

We've updated and improved 13 of our bestselling titles in line with the new Standards for QTS (September 2007). These titles are highlighted with a * in the list below.

Assessment for Learning and Teaching in Primary Schools
Mary Briggs, Angela Woodfield, Cynthia Martin and Peter Swatton
£15   176 pages   ISBN: 978 1 90330 074 9

Assessment for Learning and Teaching in Secondary Schools
Martin Fautley and Jonathan Savage
£16   160 pages   ISBN: 978 1 84445 107 4

*Learning and Teaching in Secondary Schools (third edition)
Viv Ellis
£16   192 pages   ISBN: 978 1 84445 096 1

Learning and Teaching Using ICT in Secondary Schools
John Woollard
£17.50   192 pages   ISBN: 978 1 84445 078 7

Passing the ICT Skills Test (second edition)
Clive Ferrigan
£8   80 pages   ISBN: 978 1 84445 028 2

Passing the Literacy Skills Test
Jim Johnson
£8   80 pages   ISBN: 978 1 90330 012 1

Passing the Numeracy Skills Test (third edition)
Mark Patmore,
£8   64 pages   ISBN: 978 1 90330 094 7

*Primary English: Audit and Test (third edition)
Doreen Challen
£9   64 pages   ISBN: 978 1 84445 110 4

*Primary English: Knowledge and Understanding (third edition)
Jane Medwell, George Moore, David Wray and Vivienne Griffiths
£16   240 pages   ISBN: 978 1 84445 093 0

*Primary English: Teaching Theory and Practice (third edition)
Jane Medwell, David Wray, Hilary Minns, Vivienne Griffiths and Liz Coates
£16   208 pages   ISBN: 978 1 84445 092 3

*Primary ICT: Knowledge, Understanding and Practice (third edition)
Jonathan Allen, John Potter, Jane Sharp and Keith Turvey
£16   256 pages   ISBN: 978 1 84445 094 7

*Primary Mathematics: Audit and Test (third edition)
Claire Mooney and Mike Fletcher
£9   52 pages   ISBN: 978 1 84445 111 1

*Primary Mathematics: Knowledge and Understanding (third edition)
Claire Mooney, Lindsey Ferrie, Sue Fox, Alice Hansen and Reg Wrathmell
£16   176 pages   ISBN: 978 1 84445 053 4

*Primary Mathematics: Teaching Theory and Practice (third edition)
Claire Mooney, Mary Briggs, Mike Fletcher, Alice Hansen and Judith McCullouch
£16   192 pages   ISBN: 978 1 84445 099 2

*Primary Science: Audit and Test (third edition)
John Sharp and Jenny Byrne
£9   80 pages   ISBN: 978 1 84445 109 8

*Primary Science: Knowledge and Understanding (third edition)
Graham Peacock, John Sharp, Rob Johnsey and Debbie Wright
£16   240 pages   ISBN: 978 1 84445 098 5

*Primary Science: Teaching Theory and Practice (third edition)
Rob Johnsey, John Sharp, Graham Peacock, Shirley Simon and Robin Smith
£16   144 pages   ISBN: 978 1 84445 097 8

*Professional Studies: Primary and Early Years (third edition)
Kate Jacques and Rob Hyland
£16   256 pages   ISBN: 978 1 84445 095 4

Teaching Arts in Primary Schools
Raywen Ford, Stephanie Penny, Lawry Price and Susan Young
£15   192 pages   ISBN: 978 1 90330 035 0

Teaching Design and Technology at Key Stages 1 and 2
Gill Hope
£17   224 pages   ISBN: 978 1 84445 056 5

Teaching Foundation Stage
Iris Keating
£15   200 pages   ISBN: 978 1 90330 033 6

Teaching Humanities in Primary Schools
Editor: Pat Hoodless
£15   192 pages   ISBN: 978 1 90330 036 7

Teaching Religious Education: Primary and Early Years
Elaine McCreery, Sandra Palmer and Veronica Voiels
£16   176 pages   ISBN: 978 1 84445 108 1

Achieving QTS Cross-Curricular Strand

Children's Spiritual, Moral, Social and Cultural Development
Tony Eaude
£14   128 pages   ISBN: 978 1 84445 048 0

Creativity in Primary Education
Anthony Wilson
£15   224 pages   ISBN: 978 1 84445 013 8

Creativity in Secondary Education
Jonathan Savage, Martin Fautley
£16   144 pages   ISBN: 978 1 84445 073 2

Teaching Citizenship in Primary Schools
Editor: Hilary Claire
£15   192 pages   ISBN: 978 1 84445 010 7

Teaching Literacy Across the Primary Curriculum
David Wray
£14   144 pages   ISBN: 978 1 84445 008 4

Achieving QTS Extending Knowledge in Practice

Primary English: Extending Knowledge in Practice
Jane Medwell and David Wray
£16   160 pages   ISBN: 978 1 84445 104 3

Primary ICT: Extending Knowledge in Practice
John Duffty
£16   176 pages   ISBN: 978 1 84445 055 8

Primary Mathematics: Extending Knowledge in Practice
Alice Hansen
£16   176 pages   ISBN: 978 1 84445 054 1

Primary Science: Extending Knowledge in Practice
Judith Roden, Hellen Ward and Hugh Ritchie
£16   160 pages   ISBN: 978 1 84445 106 7

Achieving QTS Practical Handbooks

Learning and Teaching with Interactive Whiteboards: Primary and Early Years
David Barber, Linda Cooper, Graham Meeson
£14   128 pages   ISBN: 978 1 84445 081 7

Learning and Teaching with Virtual Learning Environments
Helena Gillespie, Helen Boulton, Alison Hramiak and Richard Williamson
£14   144 pages   ISBN: 978 1 84445 076 3

*Successful Teaching Placement: Primary and Early Years (second edition)
Jane Medwell
£12   160 pages   ISBN: 978 1 84445 091 6

Using Resources to Support Mathematical Thinking: Primary and Early Years
Doreen Drews and Alice Hansen
£15   160 pages   ISBN: 978 1 84445 057 2

Achieving QTS Reflective Readers

Primary English Reflective Reader
Andrew Lambirth
£14   128 pages   ISBN: 978 1 84445 035 0

Primary Mathematics Reflective Reader
Louise O'Sullivan, Andrew Harris, Gina Donaldson, Gill Bottle, Margaret Sangster and Jon Wild
£14   120 pages   ISBN: 978 1 84445 036 7

Primary Professional Studies Reflective Reader
Sue Kendall-Seater
£15   192 pages   ISBN: 978 1 84445 033 6

Primary Science Reflective Reader
Judith Roden
£14   128 pages   ISBN: 978 1 84445 037 4

Primary Special Educational Needs Reflective Reader
Sue Soan
£14   136 pages   ISBN: 978 1 84445 038 1

Secondary Professional Studies Reflective Reader
Simon Hoult
£14   192 pages   ISBN: 978 1 84445 034 3

Secondary Science Reflective Reader
Gren Ireson and John Twidle
£16   128 pages   ISBN: 978 1 84445 065 7

To order please phone our order line 0845 230 9000 or send an official order or cheque to BEBC, Albion Close, Parkstone, Poole, BH12 3LL
Order online at www.learningmatters.co.uk